LEARNING TO FLY

LEARNING TO FLY

LEADERSHIP & PERFORMANCE IN THE BOARDROOM

ANGELA VINT,
CARLENA RECALDIN
& DES GOULD

KOGAN
PAGE

YOURS TO HAVE AND TO HOLD
BUT NOT TO COPY

The publication you are reading is protected by copyright law. This means that the publisher could take you and your employer to court and claim heavy legal damages if you make unauthorized photocopies from these pages. Photocopying copyright material without permission is no different from stealing a magazine from a newsagent, only it doesn't seem like theft.

The Copyright Licensing Agency (CLA) is an organization which issues licences to bring photocopying within the law. It has designed licensing services to cover all kinds of special needs in business, education and government.

If you take photocopies from books, magazines and periodicals at work your employer should be licensed with CLA. Make sure you are protected by a photocopying licence.

The Copyright Licensing Agency Limited, 90 Tottenham Court Road, London, W1P 0LP. Tel: 0171 436 5931. Fax: 0171 436 3986.

First published in 1998

Apart from any fair dealing for the purposes of research or private study, or criticism or review, as permitted under the Copyright, Designs and Patents Act 1988, this publication may only be reproduced, stored or transmitted, in any form or by any means, with the prior permission in writing of the publishers, or in the case of reprographic reproduction in accordance with the terms and licences issued by the CLA. Enquiries concerning reproduction outside those terms should be sent to the publishers at the undermentioned address:

Kogan Page Limited
120 Pentonville Road
London N1 9JN

© Angela Vint, Des Gould and Carlena Recaldin, 1998

The right of Angela Vint, Carlena Recaldin and Des Gould to be identified as authors of this work has been asserted by them in accordance with the Copyright, Designs and Patents Act 1988.

British Library Cataloguing in Publication Data

A CIP record for this book is available from the British Library.

ISBN 0 7494 2449 4

Typeset by Saxon Graphics Ltd, Derby
Printed and bound in Great Britain by
Biddles Ltd, Guildford and King's Lynn

Contents

About the Authors	*vii*
Preface	*ix*
Introduction	**1**

1 Corporate Governance   **11**
Scandal and misjudgement 12; Defining corporate governance 14; The importance of the corporate governance debate 18; Why is business not responding? 24; Improving standards of corporate governance 26; Ten-point action plan 32

2 The Changing Role of the Board   **35**
The impossible task? 36; Why do boards need to change? 38; The new role of the board 47; Corporate renewal 48; Setting direction 52; Leading change 59; Encouraging learning 65; The board's tasks 68; The board as a performing team 73

3 The Changing Role of the Director   **75**
The juggler of hats? 76; Perceptions of the director's role 77; The new role of the director 80; Different roles on the board 85; Knowledge, attributes and behaviours 93; Steps to help develop new directorial behaviours 100

4 New Perspectives on Leadership   **103**
The essence of the role of the director is leadership 104; Defining leadership 105; The challenge of leadership today 110; Team leadership 127; Learning to lead 129

Contents

5 Developing directors — **133**
In at the deep end? 134; Defining director development 143; Who is responsible for developing directors? 154; Personal development action plan 163

6 The Case for Coaching — **165**
'Giants who believe they are dwarfs' 166; What is coaching? 167; Why does coaching make the difference? 173; The coaching process 185; Coaching as a management style 192

7 Coaching Boards — **195**
The whole is greater than the sum of the parts 196; Organizational benefits of coaching boards 199; The process of coaching boards 201

8 Conclusion — **215**

Index — *000*

About the authors

ANGELA VINT

Angela Vint has worked as an organization development consultant and coach since 1987. She assists clients to create market focused strategies and develops the people to deliver them. She also works with individuals and organizations as an executive coach and facilitator to maximize potential and improve profitability through team building to achieve ownership and commitment. Angela has worked as a practising manager and consultant in a wide range of industries including advertising and media, automotive, building products, communications, engineering, financial services, government agencies and local authorities, nuclear, rail, software development and telecommunications.

She founded The Amargo Consultancy in 1990 which includes companies such as BT and Royal Mail among its clients. Amargo is a management consultancy specializing in cultural change, organizational development and corporate transformation through coaching:

> Our philosophy is to transfer our tools and techniques to the client, thus empowering and enabling them to do it for themselves. We are the catalysts for change so that the client learns to direct and manage – we do not do it for them. Thus ownership rests conclusively with the client, leading to a sustained culture of evolution and learning.

CARLENA RECALDIN

Carlena Recaldin is an independent consultant who specializes in strategic organizational change. With an MBA and a marketing background, her experience has developed through working in

About the authors

line management, management consultancy, change management and internal consultancy. Her sector experience includes information technology, security, electronics, nuclear and management consultancy. Carlena has a results orientated commercial approach to organizational change. She also has extensive experience of developing and leading teams responsible for implementing change.

DES GOULD

Des Gould has worked as an independent consultant since 1987, focusing on helping client organizations with strategic rather than tactical business issues. He is a highly experienced coach and works mainly with senior executives and board directors, facilitating them to solve their own problems through self-development. He is particularly interested in developing management thinking and practice and is the author of a number of articles. Des has worked in a range of industries including banking and international finance, engineering, consultancy and telecommunications.

Angela and Des have successfully collaborated since meeting in 1991. After many years' experience, they believe that while organizations generally know *what* they have to do to be able to grow and develop successfully, they often do not know *how* to go about doing it and, more importantly, often fail to communicate to staff *why* it needs to be done. As pioneers of corporate coaching, Angela and Des have been working with directors and managers of some of the UK's leading companies to address this including BT, Abbey National and NatWest Markets.

Contact:
Managing Director
The Amargo Consultancy
34 Southwell Riverside
Bridgnorth
WV16 4AS

Tel: 07000 781385

Preface

Our experience of working with a wide variety of organizations over the last ten years has shown that the single most difficult problem facing newly promoted senior people is how to make the transition from operational to strategic focus. This problem is most acute for newly appointed directors. In fact, developing strategic focus is just one of many new skills that a director must master if he or she is to be an effective member of the board. Yet, in our experience, very few people appointed to the position of 'director' are offered any form of induction, personal development or training to equip them for their new role.

The aim of this book is to provide directors with a practical approach for developing the skills, attitudes and knowledge necessary to direct their businesses towards outstanding performance. The emphasis is on *practical*. Many directors and managers we have spoken to over the years have bemoaned the absence of good, practical books that are written by people with current management experience, particularly in the area of improving personal performance and effectiveness. While they find the plethora of theoretical texts of interest, they are usually none the wiser as to what to actually *do* when they get back into the office. We are seeking to redress the balance with this book. We have focused less on current management theory and more on processes and practical advice. Our intention is to share our learning – the tools, ideas and processes that we have found work time and time again in a wide variety of industries and client organizations.

NOTES ABOUT STYLE

- We have used the masculine pronoun throughout this book for simplicity; no discrimination, prejudice or bias is intended by this.

Preface

- While this book is aimed at directors, people appointed to the governing board of an organization, we believe that many of the principles and ideas will be helpful to all senior managers.
- We have worked as line managers as well as consultants for a number of different organizations and can say that we have been there too and know what it is like at the coalface. Many of the examples and cases that we have cited in the book are from our direct experience and from existing clients.
- While the concept of coaching is not unique to us, the particular process of coaching that we advocate in this book is totally our own design. It has evolved and developed over the last ten years through observation, debate and successful application.

ACKNOWLEDGEMENTS

We are indebted to all those who helped us turn this book from concept into reality, particularly those clients who contributed anecdotal material: Rob Alderman, Independent Consultant; Ray Bush, General Manager – London Underground; John Flynn, Managing Director – Fred Perry Sportswear; Primrose McLaughlin, Human Resources Director – First Engineering; Ray Sale, Chief Executive – CIA Media Solutions; Tony Smith, Managing Director – First Engineering; John Spencer, Senior Commercial Manager – GTRM.

Also, to all the many people who have influenced us over the years and helped to shape our ideas – thank you.

Introduction

General perceptions about the practice and performance of boards of directors can be partially shaped by the companies that make the news headlines. These high profile examples often imply that many companies are led by boards of directors that are incompetent, and sometimes even corrupt or fraudulent. This is not the case. The majority of company directors are not only highly competent and diligent, but are also strongly personally committed to ensuring the future success of their organizations.

Nevertherless, there are still stories that appear in the media concerning poor corporate governance. These revelations are not confined to the UK but originate in the USA, Japan and Europe as well, making it a worldwide trend. The content of the stories varies from examples of corporate fraud on a massive scale, such as the collapse of the Bank of Credit and Commerce International (BCCI), to instances of large-scale mismanagement, as in the case of Barings, to cases of poor judgement, characterized by excessive unsubstantiated pay rises for company bosses. They also extend to areas of ill-conceived, even arrogant, commercial decisions made by companies, such as the McDonald's libel case. While the details of the stories are different, they have something in common: they are all examples of obdurate decision making and questionable judgement by directors.

The rising tide of high-profile examples of poor corporate governance is a consequence of three major factors.

First, there appears to have been a significant shift in public attitude towards business from the 'values-less' society of the 1980s. Whether the media is driving the moral condemnation, or merely reflecting it, is not clear and perhaps irrelevant. Nevertheless, there is a tangible backlash against individualism and the individual and corporate greed of the 1980s which was then deemed acceptable in the cause of commercial and economic advancement. The moral backlash has been underlined by the recent election of a Labour government. Much of the result was attributed to the electorate's rejection of corruption, 'sleaze' and perceived poor leadership. The scale of the Labour victory could be seen as a sign that they have captured the essence of the public mood shift and Tony Blair's early warnings to his ministers that they were 'here to work, not to enjoy the trappings of power' revealed his comprehension of this. The Cabinet's early decision not to accept ministerial pay increases awarded by the last government was a manoeuvre to demonstrate that the government was reflecting public opinion.

Returning to the business context, there appears to be a growing concern among shareholders and other stakeholders today that their interests, or those of the environment, are not being fully addressed by boards of companies. As Tim Melville-Ross (1997) puts it:

> ...business people are not seen to behave according to the values which most people regard as the norm in our daily lives away from work (p 3).

More to the point, shareholders are beginning to voice their concerns, as are pressure groups. The Worldwide Fund for Nature and Amnesty International publicly supported the shareholders of Shell who put forward a resolution calling for Shell to introduce rigorous standards for measuring its environmental and human rights policies (*Financial Times*, 6 May 1997).

Second, corporate governance has become an issue of competitive advantage. Poor corporate governance is now a route to organizational failure. One bad decision, or a right decision poorly explained and communicated, can do untold damage to an organization's reputation whereas, only a few years ago, it might have either gone unnoticed or been accepted unchallenged. Poor corporate governance has always been a problem as illustrated by the seemingly inexplicable collapse of some of the 'giants' of British corporate history, such as Rolls Royce in the 1960s. The difference today seems to be that we are no longer willing to accept it. A recent survey conducted by McKinsey (Felton *et al.*, 1996) revealed that, of the 100 respondents, over two-thirds of investors would be willing to pay more for the shares of a well-governed company. As one respondent put it, 'Companies with good board

Introduction

governance practices have a shareholder-value focus'. In the UK as well, fund holders appear to prefer companies that follow the recommendations of the Cadbury and Greenbury Committees.

Third, the directors of many of our companies are failing to cope with the demands and pressures that they currently face. The use of outdated responses to corporate difficulties – such as price wars – looks increasingly feeble and inadequate today. The Cadbury and Greenbury Committees were an attempt to alleviate public concern about poor corporate governance and their recommendations could be seen to have offered business a helping hand. However, the recommendations have not been widely implemented in most companies. Many listed companies, which are obliged to comply, have implemented the recommendations without seeming to understand the underlying principles (*Financial Times* 11 August 1997). The subsequent Hampel Committee, set up to review the recommendations of the Cadbury and Greenbury Committees, stated in its preliminary report that governance is a matter of principles rather than rules to be followed.

Boards of directors are failing their shareholders, the public, and ultimately themselves if they continue to resist change. Many have not recognized how significantly the role of the director has changed in complexity. Those who have, would appear not to know what to do about it. There is a deficiency in *directing* – that is, providing vision and leadership – in the vast majority of organizations. The difference between managing and directing is not well understood with directing rarely being practised.

The three developments we have looked at above also need to be seen in context. As is so often stated, the business environment has been through a period of fundamental change and, if anything, the pace of change is likely to increase in the future. The evidence of recent organizational upheaval is clear to see with many examples of downsizing, re-engineering, mergers and demergers and culture-change programmes. All of these can be seen as organizations' efforts to adapt to the market challenges they face. The development of adaptive organizational strategies and processes is, however, often too slow to match the changes in markets and technologies. The external drivers for change are unrelenting and gathering pace. The company that stands still or feels comfortable is risking extinction.

In our experience, and many other commentators agree (see for instance Kotter, 1996), while there have been some notable exceptions such as British Airways, the vast majority of change efforts in recent years have failed. They have failed in the sense that the achievements have been small and exacted at too high a price in terms of employee insecurity, fear and wasted resources. There is recent evidence, such as the government's 1995 *Competitiveness* White Paper, that the average performance of UK companies is worse than that of our major competitors (as quoted in RSA Inquiry, 1995). Although the UK economy is in steady recovery it appears that there is little improvement at the level of individual organizations when benchmarked against foreign companies. Another recent report assessing the risk of financial failure (Syspas, 1997) suggests that one in 14 listed UK companies will fail or need to be restructured in the next three years.

Why is this the case? We believe this malaise is caused by poor leadership and performance at the very top of our organizations: in our boardrooms. While senior and middle managers have experienced the changes of the past two decades, and many have adapted as a result, the essential changes at director level have been slow to materialize. This is partly a result of the fact that much of the recent thinking and activity in organizational development has been focused on *management*. There is remarkably little help and advice available to directors. No board that we know of is working to its optimum. We have yet to see a board working consistently as a team. This is not to say that there are no boards that operate effectively as a team, but it is indicative of the scale of the problem. We will argue that directors and boards need to understand their changing roles in today's organizations and, if they are to perform effectively in their new roles, that directors must address their own personal development and that of their boards to create effective, performing teams.

To be fair to newly appointed directors, many receive no training or induction for their new job. A study by the Institute of Directors in 1990 found that 92 per cent of company directors had received no training or development for their directorial role (quoted in Garrett, 1996). The role of a director is different in kind from that of a senior manager. To be a director requires changes in attitude, thinking style and behaviour. Unfortunately, many newly appointed directors view their promotion as a reward for years of loyal service and as an endorsement of their managerial style. It is a bit like taking your most successful salesman and making him the sales director and wondering why he then fails. Many directors continue to do

Introduction

what they did as managers. The result is they meddle and interfere, do not allow their successors to develop into their new roles, and become bogged down with day-to-day tasks and activities.

Directors need to have a *strategic*, rather than operational, focus. They must make the transition from technical expertise as being the basis of their power to wider influencing skills to manage and motivate people over whom they have no line management authority. Directors must also understand the implications of their new legal and financial responsibilities. Directors have to learn how to direct – how to be *leaders*. They are responsible for corporate transformation; that is, the ongoing development and renewal of their organization. It is not good enough to make a superior stagecoach if the latest innovation is the car!

We believe that in order to achieve corporate transformation, directors have to learn to think and behave in totally new and exciting ways. They need to embrace the need for personal transformation and learning. Ultimately, organizations are collections of people. By implication, therefore, corporate transformation requires personal transformation. If an organization is to be really successful and stay ahead, its people, especially its leaders, need to be taking risks, challenging their limiting beliefs and preconceptions and be learning all the time.

But how can directors learn the necessary new skills and behaviours? Some of the current approaches to director development suggest that there is a template or blueprint from which to work with a right and wrong answer. For instance, some corporate assessment processes are designed to identify certain types of manager who are put on rigid development programmes. However, the turbulent business environment means that no sooner is a blueprint devised than the requirements change. The process that we use extensively in our work with boards, directors and senior managers is *coaching* – a pragmatic and cogent approach to personal development. Using coaching as a methodology, we have seen remarkable examples of individual and team transformations, some of which we highlight in this book. It is precisely because coaching does not work from a template that it is so valuable in the new and emerging situations that directors now face. As no two organizations or individuals are the same, so no two coaching programmes are ever the same. They have to be tailored to meet the needs of the individual directors concerned.

What exactly is coaching? Coaching is an intensive form of personal development delivered on a one-to-one basis, between coach and client, with the objective of helping individuals to realize their full potential and a new sense of self. In this way people are better able to tackle rapidly changing organizational challenges. Coaching is all about facilitating learning on the job. It helps people grow. By focusing on the processes at work and through skilful questioning, the coach helps the director to learn in the most effective way: through experience. The person being coached takes responsibility for his own personal change and development. The coach creates the environment, using the dynamics and processes at work to guide the individual. It would be a mistake to think that this is always a comfortable process. The belief underlying coaching is that the individual has the resources within himself to solve his own problems, to find new solutions and ways of behaving, but that he needs a guiding hand and a non-judgemental ear to achieve this. It is this which directors have found so valuable: it takes place on the job, is about the job and helps them learn how to do the job better.

The process of coaching that we are talking about here has evolved and developed over the past ten years through observation, debate and successful application – it is a tried and tested approach. It needs to be differentiated from sports coaching, although there are some similar aspects such as the one-to-one relationship between coach and client. Coaching takes a broad, holistic approach that is concerned with all aspects of the individual's life and experience. Coaching is also not the same as mentoring, which tends to be a more advisory, career-centred approach often between an individual and a more senior person within the organization or profession. Nor should coaching be confused with counselling. Coaching is not remedial as it is firmly focused on creating future success, not on analysing past problems.

In this book we assert that the development of the organization is driven by the personal development of its leaders within the context of the strategy of the business. Coaching the leaders is intended to bring about relevant and focused organizational development. In our experience, it is the most effective way to close the gap between the rate of change occurring in the business environment and the speed of change in organizational and executive development. We hope to offer you a practical framework and examples to help you achieve the leap in quality required, in both personal and corporate terms, for boards to be truly leading and performing.

Introduction

THE STRUCTURE OF THE BOOK

It is all too easy in a book like this to elucidate what people should be doing with little about how this is to be achieved. We do not have all the answers, but our experience over the past ten years in many different industries has given us an insight into some practical and easily implementable approaches that will improve individual performance and effectiveness. To illustrate these, we have used a number of real client examples which we hope will demonstrate that our focus is less on theory and more on things that can actually be done. This is not to say that we are offering a sort of panacea or 'quick fix'; far from it. Our focus is on how to attain personal and corporate lifelong learning. These things cannot be achieved overnight.

Chapter 1 will examine the concept of corporate governance. It will look at the practical implications for organizations that result from the changes in expectations of public and stakeholder opinion. Shareholders and other stakeholders are demanding a higher standard of corporate governance and are growing increasingly intolerant of board level incompetence. The Cadbury and Greenbury Committee Reports offer organizations clear guidance on a new approach to financial reporting and directors' remuneration, as well as practical steps they can take. These, combined with the Institute of Directors' *Standards for the Board* offer business a practical way of improving corporate governance. We will argue that it is vital for survival that organizations listen to the public and stakeholder disquiet about corporate governance and initiate appropriate changes. Above all, this means each organization developing an approach to its stakeholders that is based on openness, integrity and accountability.

Chapter 2 will look at the changing business context for today's boards of directors. We will assess the external drivers on business and the consequences of the current business environment for organizational survival. In essence we believe that long-term survival is dependent on continuous organizational learning and corporate renewal. Thus, embrace change as a way of life and see it as a constant. Not only organizational success, but actual survival, depend on innovation in terms of the way we do things as well as the products and services we offer.

The chapter will move on to show how the need for continuous organizational learning impacts on the role of the board of directors. The board is responsible for organizational renewal and must balance this with its legal, fiscal and ethical duties. The board must be custodians and communicators, as well as creators, of the vision for the organization. At a practical level we will focus on the activities and processes that an effective board needs to undertake.

Chapter 3 will show how the individual director's role has to adapt to meet the demands placed on the board by changing market and stakeholder conditions. We will look at the outdated perceptions of the director's role and why they persist, and the difference between directing and managing will be clarified. The roles of executive and non-executive directors will also be explained. This will serve to highlight the new thinking skills and attitudes that today's directors need to play their part in a performing board.

The essence of the role of director is leadership, and in Chapter 4 we attempt to tease out the qualities and behaviours expected and needed of organizational leaders. Learning these critical elements of leadership must be a top priority for the developing director. Fundamental to this process of learning is a change in attitude. Leadership is not a job, it is a role: a way of behaving and being. People in the organization assess leadership using a variety of signals, but essentially they look to see if words match deeds and take their cue from actions. Leaders must, therefore, behave in the way that they expect their people to behave. They must act as role models and then people are more likely to 'walk their talk'. Directors are under constant scrutiny, like actors on a stage, from people within and outside the organization. These observers are constantly searching for clues and guidance for their own behaviour in that of the director. It is not easy to acquire the new attitudes and behaviours required of leadership. It starts with a passionate commitment to the corporate vision and an innate understanding of the necessary behaviours which will make the vision a reality. Above all, it requires a willingness and openness to learn, to take risks and to experiment – 'it takes behaviour to change behaviour' (Hurst, 1995, p 151). We will suggest some actions which could be 'quick wins' which, when combined with a new way of thinking, should help to set the scene for learning to be a leader.

Chapter 5 assesses the various methods available to train and develop directors to bridge the gap from manager to director. It will examine the roles of the chairman and managing director in relation to the induction, development, recruitment and selection of directors and the development of the board into an effective working team. Essentially, rather than leaving it to chance, the recruitment and induction of directors needs to be a conscious and planned process to ensure that new members are included in the social grouping of the board as early as possible so that they can be effective immediately. This avoids the newcomer 'learning' potentially divisive behaviour in order to 'fit in' with the established members of the board. As a board of directors each individual is equally responsible in law for the governance of the company. By implication, the board have collective responsibility. To carry out their responsibilities effectively the whole board must be aware of the dynamics of the group and address *how* they all work together as much as *what* they work on.

Chapter 6 will suggest that of the many ways of developing directors, among the most effective is coaching. The coaching process will be examined in detail including sharing many of our diagnostic tools and techniques. We will show how coaching can help individuals and whole organizations through enormous change in a planned, safe and managed way. The results will be verified by a number of case studies and examples.

Finally, in Chapter 7, we show how the methodology and techniques of coaching can be applied to whole boards. If the boards of directors of our organizations are going to learn to lead and perform at a superior level, director development must be set in context. The purpose of board development is to unlock the latent potential within the team and create alignment between personal and corporate aspiration, thus harnessing the full commitment and creative energy of the directors. The result will be clarity of personal and corporate visions, inspired leadership and more effective directing of the organization. Relationships both inside and outside the board will improve and be based on the principles of openness, trust and fairness. Better communication offers other people in the organization a more cohesive mental map to follow so that corporate becomes congruent and, more important, aligned. Coaching boards result in increased energy, a commitment to the team and a common purpose, greater self and team confidence and a group of people who are clearly all pulling in the same direction.

References

Felton, R F, Hudnut, A and van Heeckeren, J (1996) 'Putting a value on board governance', *The McKinsey Quarterly*, no 4, pp 170–75

References

Financial Times (1997) 6 May

Garrett, B (1996) *The Fish Rots From the Head*, HarperCollins Business, London.

Hurst, D K (1995) *Crisis and Renewal. Meeting the Challenge of Organizational Change*, Harvard Business School Press, Boston, MA

Kotter, J P (1996) *Leading Change*, Harvard Business School Press, Boston, MA

Melville-Ross, T (1997) 'Is there honour among chiefs?', *Director*, April

RSA Inquiry (1995) *Tomorrow's Company*, 6 June, p 1

Syspas (1997) *The Health of Corporate UK*, 14 April, as quoted in the *Financial Times*

Chapter 1

Corporate governance

SCANDAL AND MISJUDGEMENT

The issue of the governance of our companies is under the spotlight. While they are the exception rather than the rule, there have been examples of boardroom inadequacy, fraud, corruption, socially unacceptable decision making and 'fat-cat' directors' salaries which have prompted a public debate about corporate governance.

What may have started as media hype has now grown to involve shareholders, the public and professional bodies. Once excused as part and parcel of being in business, boardroom errors have reached new heights, which the public is finding unacceptable. Scandals such as those centring on BCCI, the Maxwell pension fund and Barings, although clearly exceptions, have been too significant to ignore. Furthermore, the handling of some of the recent privatizations has been seen as contentious in that directors have received huge gains from share options, benefiting from an increase in share price that had nothing to do with their personal performance. In addition, the lack of effective accountability in company reporting, and the lack of transparency in matters of financial disclosure have been highlighted by some sudden and large-scale corporate failures.

As we will demonstrate, the decisions being made by boards of directors in the cause of satisfying shareholders' interests are becoming increasingly inappropriate and out-of-step with public opinion and, more significantly, with shareholder opinion. Shareholders are now looking for long-term value as well as short-term returns. Boards that are perceived to be misusing company resources for short-term gain are not satisfying their governance responsibilities. The heart of the current corporate governance debate is that shareholders must believe that directors are making decisions for the good of the organization rather than for reasons of self-interest, which would be an abuse of their position as 'stewards' of companies.

Attempts to raise the standards of corporate governance have come from many directions. The Cadbury Committee Report on *The Financial Aspects of Corporate Governance* (Report of the Committee, 1992) was an attempt by the Financial Reporting Council, the London Stock Exchange and the accountancy profession to respond to the growing lack of confidence in financial reporting and auditing. As Sir Adrian Cadbury remarks in the Report's preface, '...the Committee has become the focus of far more attention than I ever envisaged', reflecting 'a climate of opinion which accepts that changes are needed...' (p 9). This was followed by a study group, set up by the CBI under the chairmanship of Sir Richard Greenbury that reported in July 1995, which looked at directors' remuneration (Report of the Study Group, 1995). At the same time, the Institute of Directors (1995) published its *Standards for the Board*, which was its attempt to contribute to the debate by clarifying the roles and responsibilities of the board.

Various elements of the business community itself have urged their colleagues to raise standards of corporate governance. In March 1997, the Institute of Directors published a report urging restraint in the area of directors' pay suggesting that 'companies need to pay more attention to ensuring directors' compensation packages can be justified by performance and by comparison with similar industries' (Lea, 1997). Subsequently, the Institute of Directors has launched various initiatives, such as encouraging business leaders to speak on values, in an effort to improve the image of business. At the Institute's 1997 annual convention, its director general Tim Melville-Ross, spoke of the damage done to the image of business by some companies not behaving with honesty and integrity. Stuart Hampson, chairman of the John Lewis Partnership, also spoke at the convention of the need to narrow the gap between the salaries for top executives and the majority of employees, stressing that 'the success of a business doesn't just result from brilliance in the boardroom' (*Financial Times*, 24 April 1997). Such efforts could be seen as a recognition by business itself that things may now have gone too far.

Most recently, the debate about corporate governance has widened from issues of financial accountability and directors' pay to issues of social accountability. The secretary general of Amnesty International, Pierre Sané, has publicly urged environmental and human rights pressure groups to enter into a dialogue with businesses in order to exchange views. Perhaps of greater significance is the increasing effectiveness of PIRC (the Pensions and Investments Research Consultancy), the corporate governance pressure group, in furthering 'the debate about corporate governance by promoting discussion', as Sir Adrian Cadbury (*Financial Times*,

1 May 1997) puts it. PIRC's aim is to promote socially responsible management through raising standards of corporate governance and making directors conscious of their responsibilities on environmental and human rights issues. PIRC has had some notable successes, including helping to ensure that Hanson did not amend its articles of association so as to limit its shareholders' voting rights. Opponents of PIRC suggest that it has not been successful in more high-profile areas, such as persuading British Gas shareholders to pass a resolution criticizing the levels of the directors' pay. Nevertheless, there is no doubt that the affair served to damage significantly British Gas's reputation.

Corporate governance, then, is a critical issue for directors. But what exactly do we mean by corporate governance and why is it so important that companies address it now? Some companies are making positive efforts to respond to the challenge of raising standards of corporate governance. So why are other companies not responding to the challenge? Is it due to a lack of understanding about the issue or is it deliberate? The remainder of this chapter will seek to answer these questions. It will also suggest a plan of action for companies intent on raising their own standards of governance.

DEFINING CORPORATE GOVERNANCE

The term *corporate governance* refers to the processes by which companies are directed and controlled. It includes the fiduciary, legal, regulatory and ethical responsibilities of the organization as well as health and safety obligations, adherence to Codes of Practice, financial reporting and auditing responsibilities and so on. The role of the shareholders in corporate governance is to elect the directors and auditors. They also need to assure themselves that the system of governance in place is appropriate and effective. The shareholders are the members of a company and the board of directors acts as their stewards.

The board of directors governs the company. It is solely responsible for the company's affairs: it cannot delegate this responsibility. In law, all directors are equally responsible for the company's affairs regardless of their technical function, their level of seniority or whether they hold an executive or non-executive position. The board's tasks include setting overall company direction, providing leadership, supervising management and reporting to shareholders and other interested parties on their stewardship. In practice, boards generally delegate the management tasks of enacting policy to produce required results to the executive directors through the managing director. But the ultimate responsibility remains the board's and it must, therefore, monitor the managing director's activities closely.

Directors' responsibilities are owed to the company, a separate legal entity or person, and not to the shareholders, although boards must have due consideration for the interests of shareholders and other parties, including potential shareholders, employees, customers, suppliers and society. At the same time directors must comply with over four hundred laws concerning their liabilities and responsibilities (Garrett, 1996, p 122) to these parties. While generally not liable for the company's debts, directors can be personally liable if they act improperly or illegally. It is all about balancing performance and compliance. The law and other regulations exist to control the potential power of the board and protect the rights of individuals affected by the board's actions. This is the theory. In practice, the 'system' still relies on the willingness of boards to comply and on shareholders using their power to dislodge the directors when they do not.

If we seem to be labouring this description of the corporate governance responsibilities of directors we make no apology. It is our experience that newly appointed directors are almost completely unaware of their official responsibilities, underlying the need for some kind of formal induction. The directors we know are usually initially overwhelmed by the legal and regulatory framework they must operate within. They often believe they are protected by limited liability when it is the shareholders, or owners, who are protected up to the limit of their paid-up shares. They are usually unaware, frequently a shock for a new non-executive director, that all directors are equally responsible for the affairs of the company. Ignorance is no excuse under the law. It is the duty of any director to report any wrong-doing. The Barings fiasco underlines this point. The City watchdog, the Securities and Futures Authority (SFA) banned one of the Barings' board, Ian Hopkins, from acting as a director despite the fact that he had flagged his concerns about Nick Leeson's cash calls in internal memos and to the bank's auditors. The SFA said that directors had a duty to persist with their concerns until they are noted by the appropriate authorities.

Learning to fly

We strongly recommend that all directors, but especially those newly appointed, acquaint themselves with their corporate governance responsibilities. One very useful document for this purpose is the Institute of Directors' (1995) *Standards for the Board*, which includes a summary of directors' main legal duties and liabilities. As one managing director we work with put it when he was inducting his new board of directors, '(they) were a bit taken aback when they realised what their responsibilities, legal and otherwise, entailed. One or two of them said "I don't see any point being a director"'.

The sphere of directors' accountability is widening. The debate about corporate governance is no longer confined to issues of voting rights and disclosure. It has moved on to incorporate issues such as product liability (for instance, the spate of prosecutions against tobacco manufacturers in the USA) and environmental and human rights (for instance the use of child labour in India by sports equipment manufacturers). It seems that companies are being expected to demonstrate that they have a social conscience. As Garrett (1996) puts it,

> ...the issue is that boards have now got to be much clearer about their values and ethics and more aware of, and skilful in their use of, the new media technologies to be openly accountable. This demands a more holistic approach by the board to the range of accountability issues, in particular the board's quality of thinking, its ethics and values, its obediency to the law and the consistency of its behaviours to its stakeholders define its approach to accountability.

Recent events at Royal Dutch/Shell serve to illustrate the point.

Case I – Royal Dutch/Shell

1995 was a difficult year for Shell with its reputation being severely damaged by two widely publicized events. First the company faced criticism of its activities in Nigeria following its silence over the lack of support for minority rights' activists, which was interpreted as support for the Nigerian government's actions. Second, there was a huge outcry in Europe, provoked by Greenpeace, about its plan to sink the Brent Spar oil storage installation in the Atlantic Ocean.

As a result of these events, Shell re-evaluated its environmental strategy. It decided it would consult non-government organizations (NGOs), such as environmental and human rights groups, in future sensitive projects in developing countries. On 17 March 1997 Shell published a statement of business principles that outlined its new approach to environmental and human rights. When launching the initiative, John Jennings, Chairman of Shell Transport and Trading, acknowledged that the company had become inward-looking, 'a state within a state' and had not been listening. The company now took the view that it needed to spot social issues before they turned into crises.

Yet, in spite of this public olive branch, Shell's reputation has continued to come under attack on its environmental and human rights record. A minority of its shareholders (representing 1 per cent of the shares of Shell) supported by PIRC, put forward a special resolution at Shell's annual general meeting on 14 May 1997 demanding an improvement in its environmental practices and business ethics in response to its handling of the two incidents just described. Specifically, 'PIRC wants Shell's national operating companies to prepare detailed reports on their compliance with environmental and corporate responsibility standards' (*Financial Times*, 2 April 1997). In effect, the dissident shareholders were not convinced that the steps Shell had taken to tighten internal controls and make more information available were sufficient. They wanted an independent review and audit procedure for Shell's environmental and human rights policies. For its part, Shell felt that its internal procedures were appropriate and that, if the shareholders were not satisfied with the directors' performance, they could vote them off the board. To compound problems for Shell, the special resolution was publicly supported by The Worldwide Fund for Nature and Amnesty UK.

In the event, Shell unsurprisingly defeated the resolution. It had won the battle, but did it win the war? Without wishing to blow the episode out of proportion, it does raise a number of important points:

1. While the share price has not been unduly affected, there can be no doubt that the episode has done Shell's reputation no good in the eyes of the public.

Learning to fly

> 2. In an effort to fend off the resolution, Shell conducted an extensive public relations campaign that included visiting its top 50 shareholders to convince them that it was already addressing the concerns raised. The fact that this dialogue had even taken place was viewed as a victory by PIRC.
> 3. As far as PIRC was concerned, even defeat was acceptable because it has brought useful publicity and public pressure.
> 4. Shell argued that it agreed with the objectives of the resolution but could not endorse it because the responsibility for policy belonged to the board. In this way it effectively muddled the issue with the process in such a way as to turn the resolution into a vote of no confidence for the board which would, of course, be defeated. While it can be accused of not helping matters by taking an aggressive stance, Shell was right to highlight the function of a board. It is not a parliament to represent each of the stakeholder interests. Yet, Shell does have other responsibilities over making profit and the only forum at which directors are accountable for these, and then only with huge shareholder support, is the annual general meeting.

THE IMPORTANCE OF THE CORPORATE GOVERNANCE DEBATE

We believe that the discussions and changes taking place in the arena of corporate governance are too significant to be ignored by organizations, whether large or small. Boards need to assess the debate and incorporate it into their strategic deliberations.

Corporate governance has become a political issue, with a capital and small 'P'. The pressure to improve standards of governance in organizations is worldwide and not confined to any one group of lobbyists. Governments, the public, pressure groups, shareholders, financial institutions and business leaders themselves are all adding their voices to persuade companies to smarten up their act. The widespread nature of this pressure points to a cultural change in societal values which some organizations are struggling to reflect.

The boundary of accountability of organizations is becoming

wider and less well-defined. Do companies have a social obligation? Should they be accountable for environmental and human rights, for instance? Where do we draw the line? It certainly seems that environmental considerations, in particular, are being seen as part of good corporate governance. Derek Higgs, chairman of Prudential's portfolio management arm, has said that how well companies manage their environmental risk will eventually be reflected in the interest rate they pay on capital (*Financial Times*, 13 May 1997). John Kay (1997), writing in the *Financial Times* about Shell says:

> The right answer is that Shell has responsibilities that extend beyond those it has to its shareholders. Shell – and any other leading company – is obliged to consider the environment and to respect human rights, and that obligation is there whether or not that consideration and that respect increases earnings per share.

He goes on to say that this does not imply that Shell should become altruistic – its purpose is not to protect the environment or champion human rights. It is an oil company. It does mean, however, that Shell must balance and trade-off all the conflicting demands and expectations. This includes, for example, the need to make good profits for the shareholders, the need to cultivate a fair and safe environment for employees and the need to consider the impact of its actions on the environment and human rights.

The corporate governance task has become more complex, demanding clear leadership and direction from boards of directors so that organizations do not become tangled in the process of trying to please all the parties all of the time. The likely outcome of this would be paralysis through fear of upsetting any one group. Many organizations are, at the moment, substituting clear strategic thinking and boardroom direction with short-term focus justified in terms of protecting shareholder interests. The interesting point here is that boards make assumptions about what their shareholders want without actually asking them and are increasingly making the wrong assumptions. The effect of focusing on shareholder return is that companies may be bringing in substantial short-term profits at the expense of tackling some of the underlying problems of the business. The water companies are a good example of this. There is a perception reflected in the media that the water companies are neglecting much-needed investment in the water infrastructure, demonstrated by the high levels of leakage, in favour of maximizing short-term returns. Certainly the companies have little incentive since customers have no choice about where to buy water but, in the long-run, we suggest this strategy may be short-sighted.

There is a growing body of evidence to support the view that good corporate governance is more than an issue of good practice – it is an issue of competitive advantage. Kleinwort Benson has found that companies adopting an inclusive approach substantially outperform the stockmarket index as a whole. Companies that have adopted an inclusive approach include The Co-operative Bank where the focus is on developing relationships with employees, customers, staff, suppliers and the community at the same time as maximizing their financial performance. A study in the USA involving 50 investors and 69 chief executives concluded that good corporate governance made a difference that investors would be willing to pay for. Taking the whole survey group, including those who would *not* be willing to pay more, the average premium was 11 per cent. As the survey's authors argue:

> An 11 per cent increase in share price would equate to an increase in earnings before interest and tax of 11 per cent in perpetuity. To put that figure into perspective, consider the scope and intensity of effort that would be required to earn a similar increase through measures such as cost cutting or higher productivity (Felton *et al.*, 1996).

There appear to be three reasons why investors will pay more for good governance:

1. they believe that a company with good governance will perform better over time and so has long-term potential;
2. they see good governance as a way of reducing risk;
3. they regard the interest in good governance as a fad but participate because well-governed companies are worth more today as corporate governance is a 'hot' topic.

As one chief executive officer (CEO) was quoted as saying, 'Good corporate governance is somewhat akin to headlights on a car. If these two companies are in a daytime race – nothing goes wrong… If the race goes past dusk, however, the company with good governance has the headlights to deal with the problem' (Felton *et al.*, 1996).

There is also evidence from the USA that companies that pay excessive salaries to their chief executives typically perform badly in terms of profitability and share price (Core *et al.*, 1997). A study by the Wharton Business School found a statistical link between chief executive pay and weak boards of directors. The authors conclude that this does not mean that high salaries are the cause of poor performance, but that they are a symptom of deeper governance problems. Another USA survey found that high salaries for top executives damage company performance by undermining employee morale (*Financial Times*, 16 April 1997).

The number of instances of shareholders taking a stand against decisions made by their boards of directors appears to be on the increase. Rather than entering into a constructive dialogue, the response of boards so far has tended to be defensive and outdated, probably reflecting an attitude of mind that the board knows best. In the example of Interflora below, the fight between shareholders and the board threatens the very survival of the company.

Another good example of the rise of 'shareholder democracy' was demonstrated at Commercial Union. Here the issue was about the right of shareholders to vote on the annual report and accounts. While this is not a legal requirement, about 97 per cent of large public companies do grant shareholders the opportunity to vote. It is seen by many as an important factor in company accountability, providing shareholders with an opportunity to pass comment on the effectiveness of the directors' stewardship during the year.

Case 2 – Interflora

Interflora, the 74-year-old association of independent florists, has recently suffered intense competition from supermarkets and petrol stations. In an attempt at corporate renewal, the board of Interflora proposed a series of measures which included turning the organization into a limited company with shares distributed to members, and a possible flotation. It also proposed to raise significantly the annual subscription paid by members while lowering the cost of individual transactions. A number of members were incensed about the proposed changes and narrowly voted, at an extraordinary general meeting, to remove the entire board. The members were angry because they felt the board was more interested in selling the company than in serving its members.

Only a few days later, another group of members demanded a postal ballot in an effort to reinstate the old board. They argued that only 950 of the 2600 members were at the meeting that deposed the board. In addition they were angry at the new board's refusal to ratify its appointment with a ballot. At the heart of the battle was organizational renewal. The old board put forward radical proposals without entering into a dialogue with its members many of whom, believing that their livelihoods were being undermined, reacted in a predictable way.

This extraordinary battle is interesting for showing the potential power of owners, members or shareholders to overthrow board decisions. However, it also shows that this is potentially to the detriment of the company as it could be argued that the changes the Interflora board were proposing were essential to the organization's future survival. It illustrates how essential it is that boards of directors engage in sensible and constructive dialogue with all stakeholders, including shareholders.

Case 3 – Commercial Union

In the past, Commercial Union has followed standard practice and offered its shareholders the chance to pass a resolution formally adopting the annual report and accounts. It took the decision, for the 1996 report and accounts, not to allow a vote on the accounts as a whole but on selected aspects, such as dividends. Commercial Union's argument for the change was that it intended to send shareholders only a summary of the report and accounts the following year and it would not be appropriate in future to ask shareholders to vote on a document that they had not seen. The company faced immediate criticism from shareholders who threatened to vote against the re-election of the chief executive, John Carter. Faced with this level of opposition, Commercial Union's board immediately retracted the decision and, at the annual general meeting, John Carter apologized to the shareholders, calling the decision 'an error'.

> One shareholder noted ironically that the long statement in the report on corporate governance should have been directed at the board itself rather than the shareholders.

The push by shareholders and other stakeholders for better standards of corporate governance will lead to greater transparency and disclosure of company results, policies and strategies. This trend has been initiated via the recommendations of the Cadbury and Greenbury Committees, in particular. These relied primarily on voluntary compliance with codes of practice. Adoption of the recommendations to date has been piecemeal and mainly confined to listed companies. There is an argument to say that if take-up of such recommendations is too slow, and standards of corporate governance are not perceived to have improved, political intervention on behalf of the public is likely.

It is difficult to ignore the message to improve standards of corporate governance when it is being advocated by business itself. The Institute of Directors, for instance, is a clear advocate of improved standards. In addition, companies must be cognisant of the power of media coverage to damage corporate reputations. As the above examples show, companies that are making corporate governance mistakes are not given an easy ride in the media.

WHY IS BUSINESS NOT RESPONDING?

Given the significant support for change in the governance of our organizations, why is it that most companies are not taking the need for change seriously? Nor is the 'head-in-the-sand' approach confined to small and medium sized companies, as we have already seen from some of the examples. The gap between public and stakeholder expectations and the behaviour of boards of directors continues to widen.

The way that the recommendations from the Cadbury and Greenbury Committees have been adopted clearly shows that business attitudes have not changed. Both committees were set up in response to public discomfort over standards of corporate governance. Both committees consulted widely. While no set of recommendations is ever perfect, the output from both committees was generally well received and felt to be practical, relying on a voluntary code of practice with which only listed companies were obliged to comply. Critics of the reports cited the extensive and arduous nature of the recommendations, suggesting that the committees had gone 'too far'. This may be true, but the critics missed the fundamental point. Both committees were recommending a change of attitude within business towards its public accountability. The Cadbury Report states that the recommended Code of Practice is based on the principles of openness, integrity and accountability. It also states that companies should 'give precedence to substance over form'. In other words, the aim should be to meet the spirit of the code rather than the letter.

The Cadbury Report generated a great deal of dialogue. Most public companies have attempted to comply with the Code of Best Practice although many could be accused of complying with the letter rather than the spirit. In some cases the overall effect is that the typical annual report has page upon page of detail while little else has changed. In other words, changes have been made technically because the companies have to comply but there is little real change in the standards of corporate governance. For instance, while there is more widespread use of non-executive directors, companies are tending to trawl them from the same pool. Also, we are likely to recruit people like ourselves with the same type of background which tends to reinforce our existing perspectives. The intention behind the Cadbury recommendation that boards should have a minimum of three non-executive directors was in an effort to raise standards of corporate governance by improving the 'independence of judgement'. Clearly, if companies are merely recruiting 'more of the same' they are missing the point.

Having said this, some of the Cadbury recommendations have been wholeheartedly endorsed in spirit and letter, particularly the need to split the chairman and chief executive roles. This has become standard practice in large companies. As a result of Greenbury we are also seeing remuneration committees being established run by non-executive directors. Nevertheless, the changes recommended by Cadbury and Greenbury (and others) are generally being introduced slowly and principally in the largest companies which are obliged to comply. In our experience, little is known about the recommendations in small and medium sized companies with compliance restricted to those that are more enlightened.

We believe that the fundamental point that has been missed by boards and authorities alike is that no specific link is being made between the performance of the board and corporate governance. If boards were truly committed to complying with the spirit of Cadbury and improving corporate governance standards, they would set and measure themselves against performance criteria. Yet in many organizations, all levels of the company, *except* the board, have performance targets.

So why is there such reluctance on the part of business to improve standards of corporate governance? We think there are five main reasons:

1. *It's just a fad* – There is a view among many directors that the current debate about corporate governance is just the latest management fashion perpetuated by the media, politicians and academics which will soon disappear. Many directors are too busy with the 'real' problems of running their businesses.
2. *It doesn't apply to us* – Directors of small to medium sized companies, in particular, would appear to think that corporate governance is an issue only for large publicly quoted companies which are more in the public eye.
3. *We're doing it already* – This is a comment frequently used and in many cases it may well be true. However, there tends to be a gap between what directors say is important and the aspects of their business that they actually measure. Our question would be: how does your board measure its performance?
4. *Misaligned perceptions* – Many boards, and we have given some examples here, believe that their ultimate responsibility is to the shareholders and, as long as they look after them, they are satisfying their corporate governance responsibilities. They have either forgotten, or are unaware, that their first duty is actually to the company, taking into account the interests of shareholders and others. Many company directors also think that much of the current debate is wrong or misguided. This is clearly the view of the recently privatized utilities about the windfall tax, for instance. Also, the Greenbury Report showed that remuneration levels for directors in the UK are within the range of European practice but well below levels in the USA. Yet, the public perception

is that directors' pay is excessive. The point is that, to a certain extent, it is irrelevant whether a perception is wrong; what matters is that someone else holds that perception at all which, for them, is reality. For instance, public confidence in the accountability of companies is low and full disclosure with improved independent auditing is being sought. Given this perception, is it sensible to not comply with full disclosure on the grounds that you know your report and accounts are totally truthful?

5. *We do not know where to start* – In our experience there is a huge amount of ignorance about the corporate governance role of the company director. Some directors are aware of their levels of ignorance but really do not know how to begin to put it right. Others prefer to tackle the issue only if it becomes a problem – what is the point in doing a lot of work for nothing?

We hope that we have persuaded you that any work done now to improve standards of corporate governance will actually improve your company's competitive standing and ensure it is in good shape for the future. So what exactly should you be doing?

IMPROVING STANDARDS OF CORPORATE GOVERNANCE

The Cadbury Committee's Code of Practice for improving standards of corporate governance was based on three fundamental principles:

1. *Openness* – The basis for the confidence which needs to exist between companies and stakeholders.
2. *Integrity* – Honest and straightforward in all dealings and reporting about the company's affairs.
3. *Accountability* – As stewards, boards are answerable to those parties affected by their actions.

Adopting these principles as a cornerstone of all its relationships would be an excellent starting point for any board of directors seeking to improve the way they govern their company. In other words, raising standards of corporate governance is not about implementing a few new systems or procedures; it is about boards adopting a new attitude of mind and a different way of thinking.

A fundamental premise is that the organization's main purpose is continuity of existence, with profit being a successful result. Boards need to consider what this means for their organization and to whom they are then accountable. Directors are the stewards of the owners, the shareholders, but their main duty is to the company. This means that shareholders' interests remain very important, but that boards must make decisions based on the best interests of the company as a whole rather than their interpretation of what the shareholders want. This brings one to the conclusion that there may be occasions when the board makes a decision in the long-term interest of the company which may reduce the return for the shareholders who may then vote the directors off the board. The more likely scenario, however, is that the shareholders will vote directors off the board for reasons of under-performance, self-interest, complacency or poor communication.

Business has complained for a long time that its competitiveness is hampered by the short-term focus of shareholders; that much needed long-term investment is sacrificed to satisfy shareholders' dividend requirements. This may have been true at one time but is a view that is certainly inappropriate now. Shareholders are more sophisticated today and make their investment decisions on a range of criteria. They require companies to take a short and long-term view. Boards' assumptions of what their shareholders or the City want may be out of date. Rather than telling them as little as possible, companies need to enter into a meaningful dialogue with their shareholders. They will be surprised that a much broader consensus exists than they might have predicted which will lead to a more collaborative relationship.

Boards need to view all the company's relationships in a similar vein. The way businesses develop their relationships with all stakeholders will be a major key to future success. The board's corporate governance performance will, therefore, to a large extent be assessed by the way it cultivates these relationships. As the report of the RSA Inquiry (1995) *Tomorrow's Company* puts it:

> *Tomorrow's Company* values reciprocal relationships. It thinks *win-win*, understanding that by focusing on all those who contribute to the business, it should improve returns to shareholders without in any way diminishing the company's accountability or focus on returns (p 9).

Learning to fly

The Co-operative Bank is an example of an organization that is implementing such an approach.

Boards need to evaluate their companies' current relationships with their stakeholders. For instance, is your payment policy for suppliers consistent with your values? Does it help or hinder a collaborative relationship with your suppliers? Does your organizational culture value openness or secrecy; that is to say, are your employees rewarded for learning and openness or for behaviour which keeps stakeholders in the dark? Is your environmental strategy based on fending off external pressure groups, or is it a partnership arrangement based on mutual co-operation for the overall benefit of the environment? Does your company's relationship with the local community enhance or devalue its reputation?

Case 4: The Co-operative Bank

The Co-operative Bank was among the first organizations to acknowledge that its corporate governance responsibilities were widening. It launched its Ethical Policy in 1992 in recognition of its 'responsibility to invest... customers' money in accordance with their wishes'. This policy has given the bank clear differentiation in a highly competitive market with relatively little marketing and promotion. This has led to a significant improvement in performance and shareholder return. The three years to 1996 have seen record profits. Pre-tax profits for 1996 increased by 24 per cent to £45.5m with earnings attributable to the equity shareholder increasing by 29 per cent to £22.7m. The Bank has seen rapid growth in the number of new customers with over 200,000 new customers joining in 1996. The majority of new customers are attracted by the Ethical Policy.

More recently, the Bank has launched its Inclusive Partnership Approach which is an extension of its Ethical Policy. It is

> based on the belief that, in every area of our business, we have an obligation to take into account the needs and interests of all those involved in our activities, or affected by them in any way...it points the way forward to an entirely new way of doing business that will have important benefits for us all in the years to come.

The essence of this approach is an ongoing dialogue between the

> Bank and the 'seven members of the inclusive partnership': customers, staff and their families, shareholders, suppliers, local communities, society at large, past and future generations.
>
> The adoption of such an approach by The Co-operative Bank contrasts sharply with attempts by other companies, such as Shell, to improve their relationships with stakeholders. For instance, the approach is consistent with the founding principles of the Co-operative Movement established by the social reformer Robert Owen. There is, therefore, a consistency and congruence behind the strategy. It is something more than a new way of marketing; it represents the way the company thinks about and behaves towards its stakeholders. When Shell tried to launch its new environmental strategy it prompted widespread criticism and mistrust as a result of Shell's past policy of secrecy. Moreover, The Co-operative Bank has launched the inclusive partnership concept by initiating a dialogue with the stakeholder groups rather than through a promotional launch. In other words, competitive advantage may result from such an approach, but the Bank appears to be initiating it more because it believes it is the right thing to do for the long-term success of the business.

Do you gather ideas from employees about how local community relations could be improved?

Developing relationships for mutual benefit will not be easy for many organizations used to, and comfortable with, an adversarial approach. This approach is about confrontation, divulging as little information as possible, and about competition. Such a style is no longer appropriate. The futility of the adversarial style is demonstrated by the water companies. The government has threatened to force water companies that have surplus water to share it with those suffering shortages. The reaction of the companies has been hostile and there has been talk of multi-million pound compensation claims from the water-rich companies who see themselves as being penalized for doing a better job. What appears to be a sensible solution to a problem affecting much of the country will be put at risk by squabbling among rival organizations. In a rare example of co-operation and collaboration, on the other hand, the two companies involved in one of the longest-running business feuds, Strix and Otter Controls, who control 90 per cent of the market for kettle thermostats, have agreed to collaborate to fight the threat of cheap Chinese copies.

Corporate governance now is about how well the board manages the sometimes conflicting expectations and demands of increasing shareholder return while fulfilling its legal and regulatory duties, as it also considers the interests of stakeholders while paying due regard to social and environmental considerations. It is about balance, trade-offs and consistency. These may appear to be contradictory, but it is only by having a clear strategy and adopting a consistent approach that boards will be able to make the right decisions.

Boards need to be clear about the company's purpose, strategy and values and to communicate these to any group with an interest in a consistent, congruent and open way. This allows people to interpret board decisions in terms of where they fit in the overall strategy of the business which, in turn, allows them to assess the performance of the board. Potential conflicts with other groups, such as shareholders, would be avoided if boards considered in advance the effect of decisions they make on each relevant party. For instance, if the board of Commercial Union had considered the possible reaction of its shareholders to losing the right to vote on the annual report and accounts, it is likely that it would have reconsidered its decision before the issue became public.

Boards need to show strong leadership. This is critical to good corporate governance. They cannot shy away from difficult decisions or hide behind the excuse that 'it's in the interests of our shareholders'. Good leadership means understanding that each stakeholder group has the right to be heard and to have its interests considered, even though the board remains responsible for the final decision which they must show to be in the best interests of the company. One of the ways of showing strong leadership is to have the courage to talk with stakeholders regularly. Companies might, for instance, set up customer, supplier or shareholder forums to initiate communications. Many organizations, such as in the retail sector, already involve suppliers in focus groups with customers about products. Another aspect boards might consider is the fact that the quality of leadership is often judged by the way we communicate. Evaluating directors' communication styles will become crucial, with presentations and media training being worthwhile investments. Companies that ask the only available director to deal with a television crew about a crisis that has arisen are not helping themselves when that director appears awkward and defensive.

Boards need to examine carefully whether their words match their deeds if they want to be trusted. If there is a mismatch between words and deeds, people will point to what the company is actually doing.

Boards need to listen to the public's concerns about corporate governance issues and the recommendations that have been put forward by, for instance, the Cadbury and Greenbury Committees and the Institute of Directors. They need to be open to criticism and new ideas. One way to do this is to embrace fully the role of the non-executive director. This role is critical for improved corporate governance if it is allowed to function effectively. The effective non-executive director contributes an objective, independent but informed judgement on the activities of the executive directors.

Also critical to improving standards of corporate governance is the separation of the chairman and chief executive roles. The company needs to be led and managed, but so does the board. By separating out the roles, boards are recognizing this fact.

We have already seen that boards must match words and deeds and nowhere is this more urgent than in directors' remuneration. A company that states in its annual report that, 'our employees are our greatest asset' but has a bonus scheme that applies only to directors, for instance, does not appear to be behaving with integrity. In general, directors' remuneration packages are not excessive. However, companies should urgently review the way they are structured to ensure that large rewards come for superior performance which is in line with corporate strategy. They should also review the gap between average employee pay and directors' pay to ensure that the discrepancy is not unfair. There is an ice cream company in the USA that has a policy that directors shall earn no more than seven times that paid to the lowest paid worker. At its annual general meeting, the shareholders voted to let the dividends due to be paid out stay in the company for reinvestment. They felt it was sufficient to own part of a truly inclusive company.

What we are talking about is a common sense, fully integrated approach to doing business which has been found to be more effective and more profitable as a result. Good corporate governance is an issue of leadership. It is about boards having the courage to put across a consistent message which is relevant to all parties. The aim is that people will say, 'if the board thinks and acts like this then the governance of this company is in safe hands'. Figure 1 summarizes what boards must do to make good corporate governance a reality.

We offer the following plan to help boards begin to improve standards of corporate governance. It may be useful to involve an objective third party, such as a coach, to help you to assess the current corporate governance position and to maintain focus on an improvement plan.

TEN-POINT ACTION PLAN

1. Buy copies of the Institute of Directors' *Good Practice for Directors – Standards for the Board* and the Cadbury Report on *The Financial Aspects of Corporate Governance* for all directors and, when they have been read, get together to discuss – what are the implications for us?
2. Compile a set of criteria for measuring the board's corporate governance performance. These should be based on objective assessments by each stakeholder group.

Good corporate governance means:

Listen	to customers, public opinion, shareholders, employees, the local, national and international community, suppliers, pressure groups, the government, regulators, competitors and other business leaders
Learn	from the opinions of all the above groups, from the mistakes made by other companies, from reports like the Cadbury and Greenbury Reports and from non-executive directors
Lead	by setting and communicating a clear purpose and strategy, by making decisions consistent with that strategy which take the views of interested parties into account and measure your board's governance performance

Figure 1   The key to good corporate governance

3. Initiate a review of all communication material with stakeholders to ensure that the messages, language and content are consistent for all parties.
4. Identify exactly who the board of directors is accountable to in its broadest sense and for what. This potentially includes anyone who is affected by any action the company undertakes.
5. Benchmark your current corporate governance performance by reviewing the company's performance from the point of view of each stakeholder group. For instance, if I were a customer, what would I think about the company and the way the board is leading it? If I were a shareholder... and so on.
6. If not already done, begin a recruitment process to select a minimum of three non-executive directors to the board. The process should start with an honest appraisal of the weaknesses of the current team.
7. Separate the role of the chairman and chief executive. One option is to select one of the non-executive directors to be the chairman.
8. Initiate a dialogue with your major stakeholders. You might, for instance, invite an important customer or shareholder to a board meeting, particularly if you are discussing an important strategic issue for the business.
9. Appoint an audit committee, a remuneration committee and a nomination committee as sub-committees of the board comprising mainly non-executive directors. In addition, ensure that the internal control system is adequate for the board to meet its responsibilites under s.221 of the Companies Act 1985.
10. Debate, agree and publish internally and externally a statement of business ethics, or business practice, which is consistent with the principles of openness, integrity and accountability.

References

Core, J E, Holthausen, R W and Larcker, D F, (1997) *Corporate Governance, CEO Compensation and Firm Performance*, The Wharton School, Pennsylvania, as quoted in the *Financial Times*, 2 May 1997

Felton, R F, Hudnut, A and van Heeckeren, J (1996) 'Putting a value on corporate governance', *The McKinsey Quarterly*, no 4

Financial Times, (1997) 2 April

Financial Times, (1997) 16 April
Financial Times (1997) 24 April
Financial Times (1997) 1 May
Financial Times, (1997) 13 May
Garratt, B (1996) *The Fish Rots From the Head*, HarperCollinsBusiness, London
Institute of Directors (1995) *Good Practice for Directors – Standards for the Board*, IoD in association with Henley Management College, London
Kay, J (1997) *Financial Times*, 16 May
Lea, R (1997) *Directors' Remuneration*, Director Publications, London, as quoted in the *Financial Times*, 20 March 1997
Report of the Committee (1992) *The Financial Aspects of Corporate Governance*, 1 December, Chaired by Sir Adrian Cadbury, Gee and Co. Ltd, London
Report of the Study Group (1995) *Directors' Remuneration*, 17 July, Chaired by Sir Richard Greenbury, Gee and Co. Ltd, London
RSA Inquiry (1995) *Tomorrow's Company*, 6 June

Chapter 2

The changing role of the board

THE IMPOSSIBLE TASK?

The board of directors is responsible for ensuring the company's success and continuity of existence. This must be achieved within the context of the legal and regulatory framework governing companies. The board must also take account of the rights of any interested parties, particularly shareholders. The Institute of Directors' (1995) *Standards for the Board* illustrates the complexity and some of the apparent contradictions of the role.

- The board must simultaneously be entrepreneurial and drive the business forward while keeping it under prudent control.
- The board is required to be sufficiently knowledgeable about the workings of the company to be answerable for its actions, yet to stand back from the day-to-day management and retain an objective, longer-term view.
- The board must be sensitive to the pressures of short-term local issues and yet be informed about broad trends and competition, often of an international nature.
- The board is expected to be focused upon the commercial needs of the business while acting responsibly towards its employees, business partners and society as a whole (p 6).

For the board to achieve its ultimate goal of securing the long-term prosperity of the company in today's competitive environment it must see its main priority as corporate renewal. Corporate renewal is about creating tomorrow's company out of today's through the processes of organizational change and learning. The board can facilitate corporate renewal by setting the direction and context for change and by focusing on four critical tasks:

1. agreeing and articulating the organization's purpose, values and vision;
2. determining the strategy and structure to enable the organization to achieve its vision;
3. delegating the implementation of strategy to management;
4. accounting for its actions.

This is the framework for the role of the board of directors. This chapter expands each element of the role in some detail. We believe boards can truly perform when they learn to balance the two critical responsibilities of performance and compliance. These aspects are two sides of the same coin: the former is about ensuring the organization's long-term future and the latter is ensuring this is done responsibly and with due consideration of all concerned with the organization.

Achieving corporate renewal within the constraints of exemplary corporate governance requires clear leadership and direction from the board. It means the board is clear about the purpose of the business, what the organization needs to look like in the future, how it will attain its vision, and has communicated these to all external and internal groups. It also means that the board has set the organizational strategy but is allowing management to implement it. And it means that the board has embraced change as a constant evolutionary process which requires the whole organization to be inquisitive and learning. The board acts as the 'business brain' (a term used by Garrett, 1996) – the central point in the organization for the collation and encouragement of imagination, creativity and innovation. The behaviour of the members of the board provides the model for others in the organization to follow. Finally, it means that the board monitors and continually improves its own performance.

Corporate renewal is about transformation. It requires the board to challenge preconceptions; to learn to think and behave in different ways. Since a board is a group of individuals, corporate transformation relies on personal transformation and development. Far from being a 'nice-to-have' when there is time and a budget, the ongoing personal development of directors is an essential part of the board's role. Corporate renewal relies on the continuous adaptation of the organization as it learns from experience and the business environment. The only way for this to occur is if the organization's members are also learning and adapting, led by the board.

It is one of the clichés of the 1990s that fundamental changes are taking place in the business environment and that the pace of change is increasing. The development of our organizations' strategies and business processes is often too slow to match the changes in markets and technologies. We believe that it is only by embracing the role that we have just outlined that boards will be able to close the ever-widening gap between the market and the organization's ability to respond to it.

WHY DO BOARDS NEED TO CHANGE?

All members of the board share the collective responsibility for its primary purpose: ensuring the long-term success of the business through corporate renewal. This implies that boards need to operate as teams focused on directing the business towards its long-term vision. In our experience this is rarely what boards do. Many of the boards we have worked with exhibited the following characteristics:

- Collections of individuals each representing the interests of their particular vertical function or area who are often in competition with each other for resources such as money and people.
- Groups of 'super' managers who have taken on directorial duties in addition to continuing to manage their function or operational area, often leading to work overload.
- People with a tendency to hold on to information and a need to be seen to have all the answers.
- Often slow to learn and recognize the need for change.
- Stifling change in an attempt to be in control of everything.
- Being told the information that managers think they want rather than the truth.
- Protecting personal position first with the future prosperity of the organization coming second.
- Disproportionate focus on short-term financial performance.
- So busy 'doing' that there is very little time available to think.
- Blocking managerial initiatives rather than leading the organization forward.

Example 1

Many of the characteristics outlined above could be ascribed to the Central Infrastructure Maintenance Unit now GT Railway Maintenance Limited (CIMU/GTRM) when we first started to work with them. We were called in to help support key staff through the sale process and to make the transition from the public to the private sector.

CIMU/GTRM was a part of British Rail that was being sold into private ownership. The board was there to act in the capacity of 'custodian' of the company until it had been purchased by new owners. The

The changing role of the board

consequence of this was that it had no powers to take strategic decisions. Directors were very operationally focused and acted largely as super managers. However, as they were caught up in the 'due diligence' process, the company became paralysed as none of the directors was available to take day-to-day decisions. This was particularly a problem for an organization that was part of BR which had a bureaucratic culture and top-down style of management. Senior managers had very limited powers of delegated authority which they were reluctant to exercise.

The directors were frustrated by the lack of progress while the senior managers were frustrated by the lack of direction and decision making at board level. We worked with the board to help them to:

- identify what the priorities were for decisions and action;
- see how they were holding the transition process up by not communicating and delegating;
- realize that the senior managers knew more than enough and should be trusted to run the business day-to-day.

We then set up the Senior Managers Group to do this which resulted in cross-functional communication for the first time at that level. Significant progress then began to be made. For instance, an audit of mobile communications found that CIMU/GTRM was actually paying for pagers and mobile phones used by other parts of British Rail and that some managers had both. This resulted in a £600,000 saving for the company. Another investigation found that the company was paying some invoices early and that the amount of money involved was significant enough to earn interest.

The sale was made and the transition from the public to the private sector was achieved successfully. It was helped by the fact that senior managers had become more effective and motivated. A number achieved significant personal advancement under the new owners of the company.

The result of boards working in this way is that change becomes impossible. There is no context set for senior managers to give them the direction in which they should be working. There is no unifying vision, mission, goal, objectives or success measures. Also, progress cannot be measured as no benchmark is taken. As a result, a lot is done by assumption, if done at all, with different things happening in different parts of the organization. This leads to much wasted time, loss of good people through frustration, entrenchment by those who want to preserve the *status quo*, little delegation and organizational issues getting 'stuck' at board level awaiting decisions. The communication between the board and the rest of the organization is often poor, leading to low staff morale and the isolation of the board. The sort of atmosphere that is created is not conducive to encouraging people to come forward with good ideas or innovations. Many boards of companies today are unwittingly responsible for constraining their organization's performance and endangering their future competitive position through persisting with outmoded practices.

These are the consequences of boards not providing leadership or direction for their organizations. They are concerned only with the *what* and not the *why* or *how* of the business. Organizations characteristically lurch from one crisis to another with huge amounts of organizational effort being used to maintain a steady state and resist change. But change, as we will show below, is inevitable and necessary. Many boards recognize the need for change but do not know how to go about it. There is a tendency to see change as some sort of paradigm shift towards corporate Utopia: a huge step change rather than a constant process of evolution. There is a feeling that unless the organization is attempting to change, it is falling behind. This often leads to great activity and investment in change programmes that ultimately fail. The organization has focused on the *what* but lost sight of *why* the change is required and *how* it should take place.

In not focusing on the *why*, boards are failing in their corporate governance and renewal responsibilities. They have lost sight of what their purpose is as a board. Given the pressures for change upon them, including all the coporate governance issues discussed in Chapter 1, why is it that most boards have not adapted their role?

- Ironically, the major obstacle to change is success. At best it breeds complacency – 'if it ain't broke don't fix it' – and at worst a sense of being invincible.

- Many directors view their appointment to the board as a reward for their competence and performance in previous years. They, therefore, often do not see the requirement to change their approach.
- Many boards are so busy managing the day-to-day issues that they are unable to take the crucial strategic view of the business. The effect of this is that issues go undetected until they become problems or crises.
- Many directors have not developed the necessary skills such as strategic thinking, team working and leadership.

Change Drivers – The Main Issues Facing Business

We have said that the business environment is changing rapidly and that this is likely to increase. But what exactly are the economic, environmental and social forces driving the need for change in organizations? We have provided a list, by no means conclusive, but which indicates the range of external issues to which companies must respond.

Globalization

Globalization refers to the growing economic interdependence of countries as a result of increased transactions in goods and services. One of the phenomena of globalization is the development of multinational corporations, some of which have revenues in excess of the gross domestic product (GDP) of many countries. The two factors that have encouraged globalization are technology and liberalization of trade barriers. Between 1930 and 1990 the cost of a three minute telephone call between London and New York fell from $244.65 to $3.32; between 1960 and 1990 the cost of a unit of computing power has fallen by over 99 per cent; the number of countries eliminating exchange controls on goods between 1970 and 1997 has increased from 35 to 137 (figures quoted in the *Financial Times*, 6 May 1997). What are the consequences for business of globalization?

- More competition from other countries, as well as other organizations. China and India are poised to become major players in the global economy.

Learning to fly

- Increased speed of business transactions due to improved communications.
- Reduction of barriers leading to larger available markets.
- Businesses are becoming disentangled from nation states due to reductions of cultural differences between countries and greater worldwide economic co-operation.
- Possible increased political intervention into companies' global activities to prevent perceived abuses of power.

Technology

Some observers have used the term 'the information revolution' to describe the impact that technology has had on the way business is conducted. There is no evidence to suggest that the pace of technological change will slow down. The companies that use technology creatively to improve the way they do business will reap the rewards. There is, however, a risk that organizations become seduced into investing in technology for its own sake and become submerged by information. The key to competitive advantage will be how companies apply technology so that it is a means to an end and not an end in itself.

There may be a backlash against some aspects of technology which substitute human contact in business. Just to take a small example, a survey by *Real Business Magazine* (*Financial Times*, 12 May 1997) found that voicemail was the best way for a company to irritate its customers. Similarly, the expected trend towards home-based working, using technology to communicate with a small central office, has not happened as fast as many predicted.

Economic

The decision as to whether the UK will join the European economic and monetary union has ramifications for business. In theory, membership should remove the final barriers to the open flow of capital, goods and services between European Union (EU) countries. Economically the UK is in a strong position relative to continental European countries which are suffering from declining competitiveness. However, this should not be a cause for complacency.

Transport

The transport infrastructure within the UK has been criticized for a number of years. The volume of road traffic has risen to the point where the road system is inadequate and the lack of investment in public transport makes it an unattractive and expensive option. Privatization of the railways and the recent change of government may bring changes to the transport infrastructure in the longer term. The government has pledged to introduce an 'integrated' transport policy. The intention seems to be to widen the focus from one dominated by roads to one that considers road policy in context with public transport improvements. Air transport continues to grow and the liberalization of some air routes has led to increased competition with improved services and lower prices for passengers.

There is likely to be a gradual trend towards greater usage of rail transport if privatization brings the expected improvements in infrastructure and costs. Road usage is unlikely to decrease, although traffic growth rates may slow down with the introduction of traffic calming measures such as road tolls. Illustrations of these trends include the fact that British Airports Authority (BAA) has commissioned a new railway link from central London to Heathrow Airport as the road system will be unable to handle the increase in traffic caused by the new Terminal Five. Some London-based companies recently publicly bemoaned the poor state of the London Underground system claiming that it did not provide visitors to London, both business and tourists, with a favourable impression.

Politics

The change of UK government seems, at this early stage, significant in terms of the moral and ethical stance that it has taken. It is clear that the government will intervene in business decisions or issues where it feels companies are not acting responsibly. This includes publicly reprimanding Camelot, the National Lottery operators, for awarding up to 90 per cent pay increases to directors at the same time as money for good causes was in decline. The government has also involved itself with the water companies in an attempt to improve their response to water shortages. On the other hand, the government has stated that it wishes to work in partnership with business, implying that it believes in a long-term relationship based on mutual benefit.

Legal and Regulatory

We have already suggested in the previous chapter that increasing regulatory and legislative control might result if the standards of corporate governance are not perceived to be improving. Changes have already taken place in the regulation of the financial sector and the government plans to introduce new regulation into the insurance market shortly.

Attempts to create one law applicable to all EU countries which would allow companies with operations in more than one member state to establish themselves as European companies have been ongoing for 25 years. The obstacle has been gaining agreement on workers' rights between the UK and Germany. A proposal has recently been put forward which might move the process on, although there are still a number of issues unresolved. Nevertheless, the change of UK government is likely to stimulate attempts to achieve this harmonization of company law.

Labour

Among the noticeable trends are:

- more part-time, contract, home-based and self-employed working as well as an increase in unpaid overtime worked by full-time workers;
- the proportion of women in the workforce continues to rise, primarily to fill part-time positions;
- after a long period of rationalization, many companies are now having to recruit again to cope with increasing demand and finding skills shortages in critical areas, such as information technology and management (the onerous task that was by and large carried out by middle managers in their mid-40s and who were the first casualties of the recession);
- there is evidence that employee share ownership makes good business sense. The UK Employee Ownership Index tracks the performance of 30 quoted companies where 10 per cent or more of the share capital is owned by employees. Since January 1992 these companies have outperformed the FTSE by 89 per cent (Capital Strategies, 1997);
- increasing influence of membership of the EU including the Social Chapter and the minimum wage. One of the conse-

quences of the Social Chapter is likely to be the requirement for all companies with over 50 employees to have workers' councils. Currently the requirement stands for companies with over 750 employees and with over 100 in a second country.

The most significant trend, however, is the change that has taken place in the psychological contract between employees and organizations. While the change has been painful for many employees, the result of a decade of downsizing and redundancies means they now have different expectations of employers. The old paternal relationship with the guarantee of a 'job for life' has disappeared. As Figure 2 shows, staff increasingly rate development opportunities and interesting work as priorities in their choice of company. Employees are taking, and are expected to take, more responsibility for their own career development rather than allowing the organization to take the lead. In other words, the new psychological contract between employee and employer is based around a commercial contract which benefits both parties and where both share in the responsibility for business success.

There is a flip side, however. The period of downsizing has led to a general distrust of employers by employees. This comes at a time when organizations rate in employees the qualities of loyalty, trust and accountability most highly. How to recruit and retain high quality staff, then, is a major issue facing business.

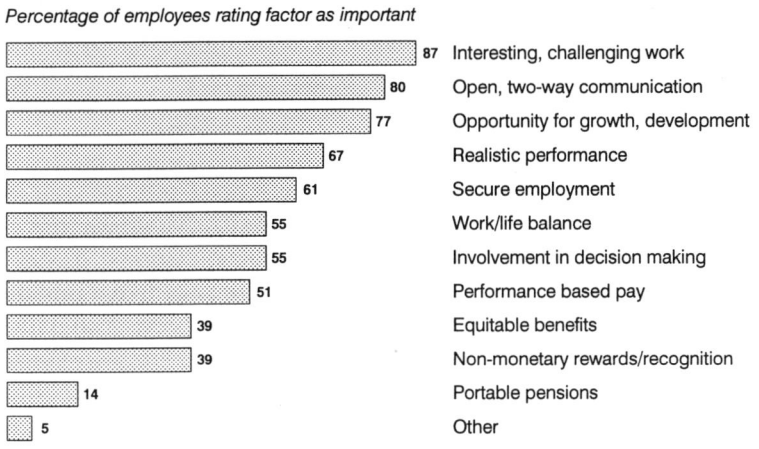

(Source: The Conference Board)

Figure 2 What employees expect from companies

Environment

For a variety of reasons ranging from improved public relations to cost savings from recyling, organizations are increasingly seeing the environment as a significant business issue. In a recent report, 47 per cent of companies surveyed claimed that environmental activities helped corporate profitability while only 11 per cent said such activities damaged profits (*UK Business & The Environment Trends Survey*, 1997). The growing corporate interest in environmental issues partially stems from pressure from public and shareholder opinion. The case of Royal Dutch/Shell in the previous chapter illustrates this point.

Social

Companies are no longer able to operate as if in an invisible protective bubble. They are expected to consider the effects of their actions on all interested groups, including the local community and general public. This trend of 'social acceptability' is likely to increase. Many businesses, such as J Sainsbury and Asda, have initiatives to support local schools. Those companies that ignore the social consequences of their actions risk damaging their reputations. McDonald's paid a high price in media attention and legal costs when it decided to pursue its libel action against two environmental activists. In the USA the government is encouraging the private sector, via tax incentives, to hire workers no longer eligible for welfare benefits as a result of reforms of the system. This is a trend that could find favour with the UK government.

Partnerships

There is a general movement towards closer co-operation and collaboration between companies and other organizations, including competitors. Most of this co-operation is driven from business necessity. For instance, the competing mobile communications manufacturers have established a joint security force to combat the rise in mobile phone theft; illustrating that some of the move towards partnerships is in recognition that all participants can achieve more by co-operating than competing.

THE NEW ROLE OF THE BOARD

As we have shown, the pressures on organizations to adapt in order to remain competitive and to survive are immense. It is the board's responsibility, as the stewards of the company, to ensure the company responds to these pressures. In order to succeed the board must first of all change the way it operates. Figure 3 pulls together the various elements of the new role of the board and shows how they interrelate. We believe that if boards focus on the *why* – the purpose, the *what* – corporate renewal, and the *how* – setting direction, leading change and establishing a learning environment, they will become performing boards.

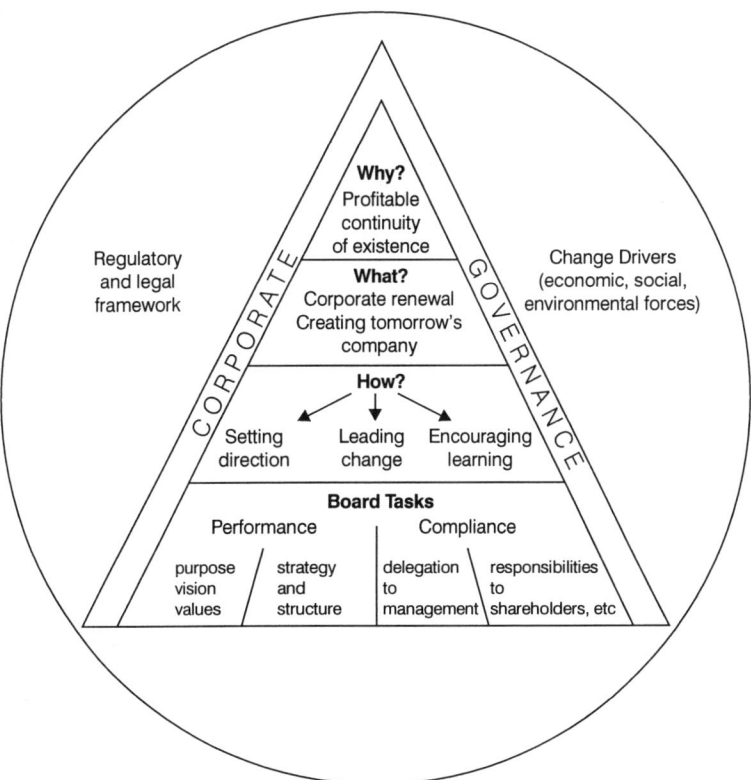

Figure 3   The complex role of the board

CORPORATE RENEWAL

The Institute of Directors defines corporate renewal as 'creating tomorrow's company out of today's'. In a sense this is all about how we become more competitive at the same time as keeping pace with new market and environmental developments. Every board that we know is engaged in trying to achieve this, although not necessarily in a conscious, structured way. Attempts to become more competitive generally stem from an incremental, operational focus rather than a strategic and innovative one.

Corporate renewal is more than just doing sufficient to keep up with others in the market. Sometimes, as we may see in the global telecommunications business, there will be no prizes for coming fourth or fifth, however big you are, but there are enormous prizes for coming first, or even second. Moreover, the rewards for companies coming first in the new product race are becoming relatively larger. There is more at stake. Take Ford's launch of the Mondeo mid-range car, for instance. So much had been invested in the product and the market was so competitive that, had the Mondeo failed, it could have brought the company down.

Renewal is about innovation and creativity. It is about a leap of imagination that transforms the way business is done or products are offered in such a way that new standards are set for the industry as a whole. Direct Line revolutionized the way insurance was offered to potential customers; The Body Shop overturned the basic premise of the cosmetics industry that women have low self-esteem by assuming that women already had self-esteem, they just wanted nice things to put on their skin (*Financial Times*, 24 April 1997); First Direct challenged the assumptions that banking transactions had to take place in office opening hours. In the last ten years or so, the companies that have contributed major step changes within an industry have tended to be new entrants: small, dynamic companies with the flexibility to do things in a new way. This is most apparent in areas of emerging technology. The interesting thing is that innovations are only new for a very short time. It does not take long before 'me too' versions appear, not least because customers' expectations have been raised. It is soon impossible to imagine life before the innovation. It is hard to remember the time before mobile phones, cash from a 'hole-in-the-wall', disposable nappies, compact discs, faxes and so on. The revenues associated with innovation are short term. The challenge for boards is how to create an organization capable of continually renewing itself.

Hurst (1995), in his book *Crisis and Renewal*, says that renewal is about changing a performance organization back into a learning organization. Turning the clock back to when it began life, in order to generate the excitement, emotional commitment and values that are often missing from large enterprises. He characterizes learning organizations as being pulled from an internal shared vision and values while a performing organization is increasingly externally controlled or constrained. He argues that constraints are an integral part of organizations. At first they help to keep the business on course, but over time they start to inhibit learning and adaptive change. Hurst argues that boards must create crises that serve to destroy these organizational constraints. He suggests that if a crisis is not created from within, in time one will happen from the external environment because the very nature of the organization at this stage is that it has become unable to respond to external change.

We think Hurst's approach is useful to consider when thinking about corporate renewal. The fact that the majority of innovations in recent years have come from new entrants lends support to his idea that companies need to be unconstrained and entrepreneurial to make major changes. Possibly this is why some large companies actually buy or create small companies to bring new technologies or innovations to the market in the realization that the existing organizational constraints would cause the new initiative to fail.

Also, being able to view crises as potentially beneficial for the long-term renewal of the business helps boards to reframe them. Rather than responding from a negative and defensive perspective where crises are seen as threats to the *status quo*, it allows the possibility of a positive, offensive approach where mistakes and problems lead to a creative energy, and hence renewal. Far more can be achieved when the mentality of the organization is as a winner than as a victim. We have seen organizations take advantage of outside forces or events to achieve necessary internal changes, such as a merger creating the opportunity to renegotiate contracts with unions. While we think crises can be a valuable catalyst for change, we would advise caution when it comes to engineering a crisis deliberately in order to transform the business. This is because there are so many interrelated factors that it may not be possible to manage them all. Managed destabilization quickly becomes unmanaged destabilization. This is certainly the case with an artificial financial crisis which can quickly drain the company of resources. We would argue that this would be an irresponsible action for a board to take.

As we have said before, however, the biggest hurdle to change is complacency. To achieve renewal when times are good may well require some form of crisis creation; for instance, by how the company's performance is communicated. As Kotter (1996) put it:

> I have seen people successfully initiate restructurings or quality efforts during times when their firms were making record profits. They did so by relentlessly bombarding employees with information about problems (profits up but market share down), potential problems (a new competitor is showing signs of becoming more aggressive), or potential opportunities (through technology or new markets). They did so by setting vastly ambitious goals that disrupted the status quo (p 46).

We have seen examples of change taking place in organizations in spite of healthy profits as a result of consistent messages of potential problems.

Example 2

One monopoly organization we have worked with has been through an enormous, largely successful, change programme designed to cut costs and organize the business around customer requirements. This was achieved in spite of the fact that the company makes very healthy annual profits and has the security of long-term fixed contracts with many of its customers. It stemmed from a request from a major customer, which was under pressure to cut costs, for a reduction in prices. Rather than relying on its comfortable monopoly position and refusing the price reductions, the board decided to comply with the customer's request for the long-term benefit of the industry as a whole. This was not an altruistic decision. The industry is an old one and in decline. The board realized that its monopoly position could not be guaranteed indefinitely. The best way for the industry, as a whole, to extend its lifetime was through collaboration of all participants.

The organization was so stable that complacency levels were high. Over a long period, the board sent a consistent message to employ-

> ees that the company's long-term survival meant satisfying customers and cutting costs. After some time, a sense of urgency was created among sufficient numbers of employees to initiate the required organizational changes.

There are examples of large organizations that are constantly renewing themselves. Virgin, for instance, continues to reinvent itself, moving from entertainment to the airline business and, more recently, financial services and even Virgin Cola. Its entry into different markets is characterized by innovation: its entry heralds a step-change for the way products are offered, such as vastly reducing transatlantic air fares. Such organizations remain true to their core purpose or style but are not constrained by it. Virgin did not see itself as in the entertainment or airline business, which would have constrained its development: it has remained true to its principles of customer service and affordability. Companies can view their core purpose or *raison d'être* too narrowly.

Example 3

One of our clients is a large building society which became a bank. However, the organization is finding it difficult to move from the mindset of being a building society. Major decisions continue to be made from the point of view of a building society, not a bank. For instance, it recently made a large acquisition of another building society. This meant acquiring another mortgage book on which it may be difficult to make and sustain profits. Had the organization seen its core purpose as providing financial services, rather than as a building society, the company might have made a different investment decision.

Corporate renewal is an area of risk and uncertainty for boards. It demands new thought processes and imagination. The board needs to learn to step out of the light and walk alone in the dark. It needs to leave the comfort of what is known and comfortable and explore the unknown. The board has huge resources and help available for this task from the organization itself. An organization's employees are a source of imagination and learning. This sounds an obvious statement but many of the boards we work with feel it is their job to produce all the good ideas. To release this potential, the board must exercise humility, learn how to listen and see itself as the central point for learning and ideas for the whole organization.

Corporate renewal is not an easy process. When your organization is profitable, has a strong position in the market and a good reputation, how do you persuade your fellow directors that the organization must renew itself and, if necessary, generate a crisis to do so? It seems to defy rational thought. However, this is the scenario that boards must come to terms with in order to achieve their goal of long-term prosperity in today's business environment. Again, it is useful to reframe the concept. If boards permanently have their eye on the future, on the organization's vision and are excited by what is possible, then the current day success can be put into perspective. It becomes just one step of a series of successful steps into the future. As Hamel (*Financial Times*, 24 April 1997) has said:

> The test for any company today is whether they can tell me the five fundamental ways they're going to change their industry in the next 10 years. If they can't, somebody else will.

The key to this approach is for the board to create the organizational context by setting and communicating the vision of the future and then establishing an environment of ongoing change and learning. In this way the board facilitates the process of corporate renewal from within. As Figure 3 showed, boards can achieve corporate renewal via the processes of setting direction, leading change and encouraging learning.

SETTING DIRECTION

When we get in the car and set out on a journey we usually know our final destination. There may be a number of possible routes that we could take, some of which might take longer than others. But ultimately, the reason that we have embarked on the journey is in order to reach somewhere. It is surprising, but nevertheless

The changing role of the board

true, that many organizations set off on their journey with little idea of where they want to end up. As we have said before, it is often the case that companies feel the pressure to change without understanding why or how, leading to activity without purpose.

It is for the board of directors to set the direction for the company. What exactly is involved? There are two elements: establishing the organization's identity or reason for existence and creating the organization's vision of the future. Outstanding organizations such as Hewlett-Packard, Virgin, Sony, Marks & Spencer, Toyota and Microsoft achieve continuous renewal at the same time as exceptional long-term performance. They have a core identity that remains fixed while their business strategies adapt to the changing environment. They develop and change yet remain true to themselves and what they stand for. The challenge for the board is to understand what in the organization should change and what should never be changed: to manage consistency and purposeful change. Figure 4 summarizes the elements involved for a board when setting the organization's direction.

Identity

An organization's identity cannot be invented. It can only work as a source of inspiration and direction if it is authentic. It is something that the board must discover through inward reflection. Companies that are clear about their identity tend to attract employees that have consistent personal values. You cannot make people share your organization's purpose and values. They are

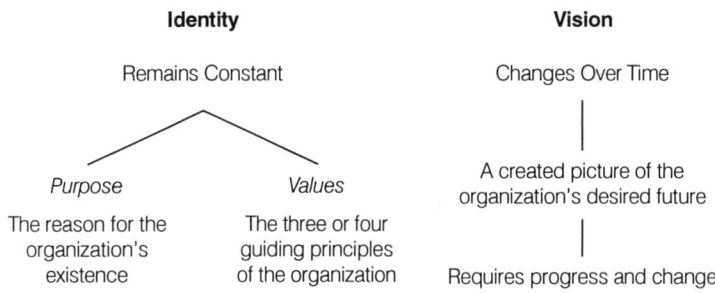

Figure 4 Setting organizational direction

something fundamental within organizations and people. In fact, when identifying and communicating the purpose and values of the organization the board may find that employees with inconsistent values may leave. This should be looked on as a positive outcome. It is important to emphasize here that many different types of people with diverse points of view can share an organization's purpose and principal values. There should be no implication of a constraining culture or 'group-think'. Some organizations do not articulate their guiding principles because they do not need to. It is symbolized by the way employees work, the layout and type of offices and the company-specific language.

Purpose

The purpose of the organization is the reason it exists. It 'provides the glue that holds an organization together as it grows, decentralizes, diversifies, expands globally and develops workplace diversity' (Collins and Porras, 1996). Hewlett-Packard is often quoted as an example of a company that remains true to its purpose; the 'HP Way'. At its heart is the belief that the company exists to improve the welfare of humanity through technical advancements. The purpose of the organization is a constant guide no matter what markets the company enters or which products it produces. So it is more about what we are than what we do. The purpose, the ultimate goal of the company, is never reached although many visions will be achieved along the way.

When trying to describe their purpose, organizations can fall into two traps. First, they might simply describe the product sectors they are in which limits their scope. Second, they might just make the somewhat prosaic claim that the purpose is to maximize profits. The latter is an important purpose but is one that is shared by all other profit-making businesses and will not, therefore, provide the business with its own internal guide that motivates and directs. Better examples of declared purposes include Walt Disney's 'To make people happy', McKinsey & Company's 'To help leading corporations and governments be more successful' and 3M's 'To solve unsolved problems innovatively' (Collins and Porras, 1996).

One method for finding the organization's purpose (Collins and Porras, 1996) is for the board to ask the 'five whys'. The board begins with a descriptive statement of what it thinks its purpose is

The changing role of the board

and then asks itself 'Why is that important?' five times. This can be a powerful way of delving beneath the surface of an organization.

Values

These are the three or four principles of the organization. They exist irrespective of company or market conditions. Marks & Spencer's values revolve around quality, value for money and customer service and have endured throughout the company's existence. Volkswagen's values are based on value for money and reliability. To put these in context, these values are so basic to the organization that there may be a time when they act as a competitive disadvantage, depending on the market conditions. There will be other values or cultural norms that the organization has which are usually expressed in terms of behaviours and which evolve with the corporate culture. These should not be confused with the core values which, along with the purpose, provide the identity or personality of the business.

To identify the basic values of the business, the board must be ruthlessly honest. It must not confuse what the values really are with what the board would like them to be. This will lead to cynicism and inauthenticity. If the board derives more than five principal values, then it has probably started to confuse those values that are absolutely key with others that are more likely to change. Once the board has derived the core values, it needs to test whether it has really found the ones that epitomize the business. One way to do this is to ask, 'If the market place changed and penalized the business for having this value, would you still hold it?' If the answer is no, then the board probably needs to look deeper to find the real values.

Vision

The vision of the organization is the picture of what the business will be like in the future. The more vivid the description, the more effective it will be in galvanizing employees to work towards the vision. The vision is an ambitious but achievable target. It is sufficiently tangible to enable goals to be set along the way. The organization's vision will vary over time depending on market conditions but will remain within the framework of the organization's intrinsic identity. Unlike the purpose which is something inherent to the business, the vision is created. This is where the organization's collective imagination and learning is exercised.

It is the board's responsibility to create, communicate and lead the business towards the vision. The board can do this alone. In cases where there is a crisis, for instance, it may be appropriate for the board to develop the vision and then inform the rest of the organization. This is an authoritarian approach which, provided it is relevant and communicated honestly and with sufficient urgency, can galvanize employee support. At the other extreme, the board could decide to develop the vision in conjunction with the organization's employees. This has the benefit that employee commitment is assured but is a more difficult process. It requires listening to all views, however diverse, treating everyone with equal respect and seeking alignment not agreement. There is the risk that people will feel that their views were ignored if their vision was not the one finally agreed.

Practically, many boards will choose a process somewhere between these two extremes to develop their vision. For instance, the board creates the vision which is 'big' or 'wide' enough to allow divisions and departments to create their own mission which is in alignment with the overall vision and contributes to its achievement. That way the employees feel involved and articulate specifically where they make a difference. Thus, the vision is strategic and the mission is operational. To take an example, the vision might be to put a man on the moon and the mission would be to build an x ton rocket that will take y people and be ready by z date.

The board has the ultimate responsibility for ensuring that the organization achieves the vision, but it can only be realized if employees are motivated by it. In consulting employees about the sort of vision that the organization should have, the board is communicating the reasons why change is necessary; a fundamental step in the realization of the vision. The amount of energy released when employees are aligned with the vision can be difficult to control. One senior executive talking about his team described coming to work as like 'trying to steer seven wild horses instead of beating seven dead horses to move' (Roberts, 1994).

A powerful vision also serves the function of motivating employees to do things that are not necessarily in their own interests. There is an explicit trade-off of short-term pain for longer-term personal satisfaction. When British Airways realized that increasing competition and falling fares meant that within a few years it would not be making any money, it put the problem to its employees. They were told that their salaries were 30 per cent above the industry average and there would have to be job losses. This was not an easy pill to swallow for the employees but they were able to see that by accepting painful change today they were assured of longer-term survival. Another powerful function served by a clear vision is that it is empowering. It provides sufficient direction to mean that employees do not have to check each decision with management.

If any member of the board cannot communicate the organization's vision in less than five minutes in a way that is understandable by anyone, then it does not have a workable vision. When creating the vision it is useful to imagine yourself within it. Imagine you are looking at the business of the future; what can you see around you, what does it feel like, what sounds can you hear? The more 'real' the vision, the easier it is to realize and to communicate to others. If you have actually been there yourself, so to speak, you are more likely to present the vision to others congruently and enthusiastically. As Kotter (1996) puts it:

> Developing a good vision is an exercise of both the head and the heart, it takes some time, it always involves a group of people and it is tough to do well.

An essential part of the vision process for the board is to create what Peter Senge and others have called 'shared meaning'. It does not matter how good the vision is, if it is not communicated and understood and employees are not aligned to it, it will not be achieved. How many times have you found yourself in the position where you think you have explained something to someone and yet they still claim that you either have not told them, they do not understand what you have told them or they have interpreted it in a different way? Imagine this multiplied by the number of employees within the organization and you begin to see why it is that we can never communicate too much. Most companies vastly underestimate how much communication needs to take place.

Change processes often flounder or go awry because employees do not know the vision. Boards that feel their employees are deliberately sabotaging a change process should ask themselves if their

Learning to fly

employees actually share the same meaning of the vision as the board. The other thing to remember is that communication is not just about words. In fact, experiments have shown that if a presenter gives one message in words and another non-verbally, the audience will remember the non-verbal message. The board member who does not agree with the vision but goes along with it for a peaceful life is not doing himself or the organization any good. It is what we call public support versus private subversion. Nothing is as powerful as an important individual spreading the message of a new vision in words and deeds, particularly if it seems out of character. The converse is also true.

> **Example 4**
>
> One member of the board of an organization was known normally to be resistant to change. He was a powerful individual in charge of the majority of the operational workforce. The board had put together an agreed vision for a significant change to the business and the individual had been vociferous in his opposition throughout. Mass meetings were held to communicate the vision to the whole workforce led by each member of the board all of whom had the same presentational material. There was a concern that the individual would undermine the process. Yet quite the opposite was true. The feedback from the meetings held by the cynical director were full of comments like... 'he clearly believes in it, so it must be OK' and 'I don't like the message but I can see that we need to change'. In voicing his discontent, the director had been going through a personal process of letting go of the *status quo*. When it came to the meetings he really believed in the vision and the need for change and this was conveyed.
>
> The feedback from meetings held by other directors also held a surprise. The feedback from one of the other director's meetings was hostile and aggressive; 'He was smug', 'I'm alright, I've got a job' and 'This is what's going to happen – like it or not'. This director had not voiced any disagreement with the vision or change but neither had he 'bought into' them. It was as if it was all happening around him and was not real. This was exactly the message that he conveyed to the employees.

Creating a vision is not an intellectual exercise and certainly can not be delegated. The board must believe in it and convey that belief through their words and deeds. The board must take the lead and step out on the route to the vision of the organization's future.

To start the process of developing a vision, it can be helpful to begin by answering questions like those below (adapted from Roberts, 1994, pp 337–8). Imagine that you are in the company five years from now and you have achieved the vision.

- What does the company look like?
- What does it feel like to work here?
- How would you describe the people who work here?
- What sort of conversations are going on around you?
- What are other people saying about the company?
- How is the company making money?
- Who are the stakeholders and what are you doing for them?
- What does the industry look like?
- What is your competitive differentiation?
- What unique contribution does the business make?
- What do you value?
- How are people rewarded?

LEADING CHANGE

Boards must accept change as an integral part of organizational life. To quote Sir John Harvey-Jones (1988), 'Without change nothing is possible. Not to change is a sure sign of imminent extinction. Whether change is comfortable or not, it is inevitable'. Much of the change that we have seen taking place in organizations over the past ten years has been sporadic, a response to an external crisis and often painful. There is growing evidence too, that many of these change programmes will ultimately fail. Generally, companies have embarked on change programmes to cope with a crisis hoping that once the programme was finished everything could get back to normal again. This reflects the pervasive wish for business to be as it used to be: rational, predictable and stable. To hold on to such an ideal is dangerous for the organization. To accept change as a natural and continuous process means that you are in control of it.

An essential part of the board's role is to lead organizational change in order to achieve corporate renewal. This means setting the context that allows the organization to evolve and adapt. We do see evolutionary change taking place in some organizations but it is generally too slow to match the change in market conditions. It needs to be more conscious and positive. Rather than an attempt to keep up with the market, your organizational change needs to be dictating the pace for the industry.

There will be times when the organization needs to instigate a step-change. A new technological development or entrant into the market may well require a step-change in addition to the evolutionary change taking place. Successful change programmes are characterized by a well-designed process for generating sufficient energy to counter all the obstacles. Also, they are driven by leaders and implemented by managers. To be able to lead change, the board has to involve itself in the design of the change process. This is not a task that can be delegated. What should be delegated is the implementation of the process. Too often boards accept the need for change and may even produce a vision. They then pass the baton or the *what* to managers who begin the tasks associated with the change. What is then missing is the *why* – the rationale and context for change – and *how* to make it happen. Part of the leadership role is to understand the change process and guide it. One aspect of this is to recognize and understand the obstacles to change.

Obstacles to Change

The greatest obstacle to change is complacency. The past success of an organization is no guarantee of future achievements. The natural human tendency for denial when confronted by bad news and fear of the unknown conspire to bring the usual response of doing nothing.

Example 5

The company had been the leader in all of its product sectors since its formation in the early twentieth century. Technological changes in the early 1980s changed the industry. Growth rates approached 20 per cent per annum. Costs fell dramatically as did prices, although

> margins remained good bringing a flood of new entrants. New products emerged which revolutionized the way business was done.
>
> The past success of the company led to an arrogance that customers would stay with the company because 'we are still the best'. When customers started to leave the response was to blame one competitor in particular for dirty tactics. No change took place within the company although the R&D department belatedly began to design some new products. Over a period of ten years the company lost 10 per cent market share in its main product sector and over half of its customer base. The company declined to the point of being just like many others in the business before it began to respond.

Another obstacle to change is an unclear guiding vision or one that has been undercommunicated. This is often the problem in change processes where the smallest of decisions seems to create a disproportionate level of debate and conflict. Everyone's idea of the vision is their own and different.

Change is generally complex and difficult and is often run as a 'project'; tacked on to managers' everyday tasks. After a while those involved become weary and just want to 'get back to normal'. If the leaders have seen a few successes from the programme they are all very likely to believe that the change has been successful and become embedded in the culture. There is a collective 'pat-on-the-back' and within a short time there is little, if any, evidence of change. The point is that change takes time and is not something that is done as well as everything else but instead of something else. The change has not occured until it has become part of the corporate culture.

Another major obstacle to change is underestimating the effect of change on individuals. This is particularly the case in organizations where a step change is needed which affects most or all employees. A model that we use frequently with clients to demonstrate the effect of change on individuals is shown in Figure 5.

Major organizational change generally requires personal change which is often painful. Many change models and programmes take no account of people's feelings. Yet people going through change go through a process akin to grief where they let go of what was and

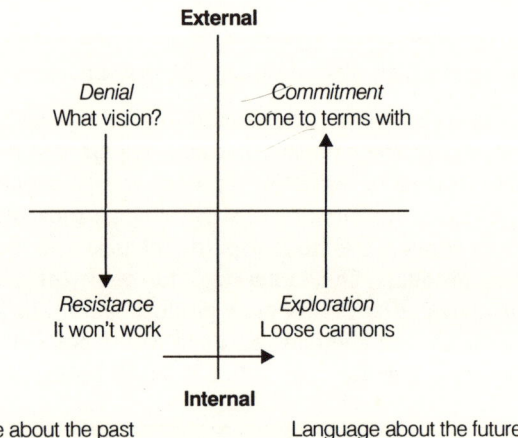

Figure 5 The change model

begin to accept what exists now. It is a process that takes time and consequently change programmes must take as long as is necessary for everyone critical to the company to go through the cycle. We actually say that change should move at the pace of the slowest essential person because if you wait for everyone it will never happen.

When first confronted with change our first response as human beings is often to deny the necessity for it. When we have to come to terms with the necessity for change but do not like it our response can be to resist. Once through resistance, we become willing to explore new ways of doing things in the new regime, new culture or new situation in which we find ourselves. Finally, we reach commitment as we accept the new circumstances. Some people will be unable or unwilling to get to commitment and will need to be helped out of the organization. A person's reaction to change is not always predictable. People can move from denial to resistance and back again. Given our different attitudes to situations, unless change is handled professionally it is by no means guaranteed that all people will move through the cycle to commitment. This is where coaching can help. Much of our work with clients is concerned with helping them facilitate themselves and their employees though change.

The changing role of the board

The change process, frustrating as this might be for the board, will move at the speed of the slowest crucial person. It will not become embedded until the last person has gone round the cycle and is committed. Vision needs to be built and communicated slowly to avoid what we call 'the Tarzan Swing'. This is where companies try to push people straight from denial to commitment. This inevitably means that commitment will not be real and within a short time the majority of people will slip back to resistance. If our discussion of personal change sounds daunting it is useful to remember that many will go through the process very quickly. Also, the process becomes far less traumatic when an organization is continually changing. This is, first, because the change is more incremental than a huge upheaval; and second, people learn to reframe change when it becomes a way of life and look upon it as a challenge and learning opportunity rather than a threat.

When putting together a change programme, like many companies we believe in identifying the 'change agents' to help manage the process. These are usually bright, ambitious people who have not only embraced the vision, but may well have helped to design it. They have recognized the necessity for the change and are energized to pull the company through it. Figure 6 shows that boards need to choose their change agents carefully.

It would be easy to mistake energy and ambition for commitment and recruit change agents from the ranks of the Saboteurs. (Kotter (1996) refers to these individuals as 'snakes'; people who deliber-

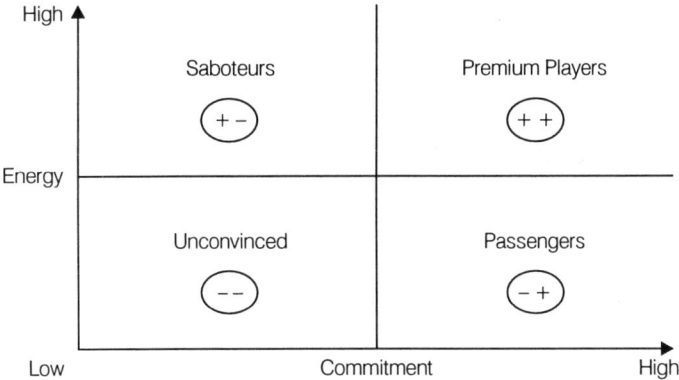

Figure 6 The energy map

ately create mistrust in order to destroy team work.) Instead boards need to choose their Premium Players. These people provide the energy for change in the organization and the board must nurture them. We have often seen the situation where people help to steer a change programme and go through considerable personal change and development. At the end of the process they are usually expected to go back to their 'day jobs'; something which most find virtually impossible. Boards need to be aware of the impact of personal change and ensure that people continue to be encouraged to learn for the sake of the organization.

Setting the Context

We have listed below some ideas for boards as to how they might begin to lead change within their organizations.

- Set performance targets so high that it will be impossible to achieve them without doing things differently.
- Circulate information to all employees that shows critical areas of weakness in the organization; for example, customer satisfaction, performance against the competition.
- Talk about future opportunities rather than present successes when communicating with employees.
- In everything you do set the example by being optimistic, enthusiatic and positive about the future.
- Constantly look for symbolic actions that you can take which illustrate to employees that you are changing; for example, closing the directors' dining room, freezing directors' salaries, setting higher performance targets for directors.
- Be familiar with the process of change. Look for and remove obstacles to change. In particular, identify the business processes, such as financial and personnel systems, within the organization that are a block to managerial action and revise them so they are not an obstacle to change and organizational learning.
- Actively listen to the messages from inside and outside the organization about the direction and progress of the organization's change – find the 'corporate pulse'.
- Think about the language you use and bring in words that indicate change, such as 'big leaps', 'vision', 'opportunity'.

- Nurture change agents but do not rely on them alone to make change happen.
- Bring in experienced consultants and/or other third parties to give you an objective, external view of how the organization is doing, particularly people who are prepared to implement the ideas in which they believe.
- Be in control of change. Actively involve employees in identifying areas of change. Measure the progress of change: in particular, use employee surveys to assess whether change is becoming embedded in the culture – 'the way we do things round here'.
- Find a partner or coach, preferably from outside the organization, whom you can trust to help you deal with the personal stress and emotional tension that results from intense periods of change. If you are leading change, people expect honesty, openness and confidence which are easier to produce if someone has helped you to work out your own feelings about what is happening.

ENCOURAGING LEARNING

Corporate renewal means being first to bring products, new technologies and services to market. To be able to achieve this sort of performance consistently means that the organization has to be open to, and looking for, new ideas. Instead, many companies are threatened by new ideas: they mean change, more work and uncertainty.

Boards need to create an atmosphere of curiosity and learning for their organizations to be able to see and develop new ideas. Many companies have been able to engender such a culture. Nokia spends a significant percentage of its turnover on R&D and has built a factory next to the largest engineering university in Finland. Learning is not something confined to the board. The board's role is to set the example by ensuring that it is prepared to learn and to establish an organizational climate which says that learning is the responsibility of everyone in the organization. This means an organizational climate where diversity of views is encouraged, awareness is heightened and people ask questions: how can we make this product better, cheaper, more quickly?

Encouraging learning sounds straightforward on paper and many organizations claim to be doing it. We believe that the reality is difficult because it challenges conventional organizational thinking patterns. To begin with, it means being able to make mistakes; not those that occur as a result of carelessness but those that have to be made when acquiring new knowledge. When a baby learns to walk, it does not just decide to do so one day and immediately set off. It spends weeks or months staggering to its feet, taking wobbly steps and falling over. And it is not put off by all the mistakes it makes but perseveres until it has mastered the art of walking. Similarly, when we first learned to drive, most of us did not sit at the wheel and immediately drive in as skilled a way as we do now: we were more likely to have stalled the engine.

The point is that many of our organizations breed a culture, sometimes referred to as a 'blame culture', where mistakes are not tolerated. This leads to a fear of making mistakes which paralyses learning. But mistakes are how we learn and how new things are discovered. 'The value of a mistake lies in the lessons we learn from it, not necessarily in the mistake itself' (Pearn, 1997). Does your organization allow mistakes? We know a managing director of one small company who gives his managers a 'mistakes budget' that can be spent as they please without any need to explain it.

When your employees present you with negative information that makes you uncomfortable, do you 'shoot the messenger'? In spite of our best attempts to be open to challenge, we very often view bad news as a reflection of our performance and reject it. Unfortunately this means that people stop telling us things that we need to know. Boards need to be aware of how they handle negative information: it is a potential source of learning. We can all think of someone who gets on our nerves because they are always putting a counter-point of view. The next time you feel yourself becoming impatient with someone like this, listen to what the individual is trying to tell you. Sometimes we need to go beyond the language used to hear the message.

Another symptom of conventional thinking is our tendency to seek agreement between people. This is difficult, time-consuming and can lead to an intolerance of different views and people. What we believe is more relevant now is to seek alignment which allows loyal opposition – 'I do not like this idea but I believe in what we are collectively trying to do because there is some value in it and we cannot carry on doing what we are doing now'.

The changing role of the board

Imagine that you walked past a director's office and you saw him talking rapidly on the telephone at the same time as trying to read a pile of papers on his desk. Now imagine that you walk past that same director's office and observe that there are no papers on the desk, there is quiet music playing and he is leaning back in his chair, deep in contemplation. What would you make of these two scenarios? Which would make you the most uncomfortable? We tend to associate activity with productivity in organizations. The trouble is that this does not allow time for thinking, which is especially important at board level. Do you set time aside in your diary for thinking? One managing director we talked to recently was sad to see that his directors were so busy dealing with the day-to-day issues that no one was thinking 'discursively and reflectively on the real issues of survival'.

Many boards feel that they are beyond learning. They are happy to encourage others in the organization to develop and learn as long as they do not have to do it themselves. It is as if now I have got to board level it must mean that I know it all. Boards must set the tone. This means all members of the board should be actively pursuing their own personal development. It also means board members must acknowledge to themselves and the rest of the organization that they do not have all the answers. Why should any small group of individuals have the monopoly on good ideas? Usually they do not know all the questions, let alone all the answers. For those of us who are naturally decisive and used to knowing what to do, this is a difficult frame of mind to adapt to. We seem to turn into human 'doings' rather than human beings!

To encourage a learning environment the board needs to begin by taking an honest and objective look at current reality. This means challenging 'sacred cows' and 'limiting beliefs'. Limiting beliefs, which we will return to in a later chapter, are assumptions we have about ourselves, our department or the organization but which may not be true. One company had a limiting belief that it was an installations company until it was pointed out that it made virtually all its profit from its less glamorous maintenance business. When this belief was challenged it allowed the company to begin to see itself as a service business which opened up new, more profitable, opportunities. It is often useful when trying to take a fresh look at your organization to remember your impressions on your first day with the company. What things stood out for you?

Learning to fly

The board needs to determine current reality to serve as a benchmark for organizational learning. It also needs to introduce performance measures and targets so that learning is relevant. It is all very well to claim that learning takes place but how do you know if you do not measure it? It is an age-old business maxim that if you cannot or do not measure it, you cannot or will not manage it. Apart from measuring customer satisfation, time taken to resolve complaints and so on, you might consider a 'new ideas register', measuring the percentage of ideas that have been acted upon. Another useful measure might be turnover of staff. We know of one manager who has lost 17 members of staff because his style is so abrasive that people refuse to work with him.

Creating an environment that encourages learning and self-development is also a way that boards can tackle one of the major issues facing business today: recruiting and retaining good staff. Loyalty and commitment from employees is now offered in return for challenging projects rather than regular promotion. But boards must not confine themselves to setting the learning context just for employees. Organizations must learn from customers, suppliers and the community by having few communication barriers and developing close relationships.

THE BOARD'S TASKS

Figure 3 showed the *why, what* and *how* of the board's role. It also showed four areas of board activity. These are critical actions that boards need to undertake which help to facilitate the processes of direction setting, leading change and encouraging learning. They are also vital for ensuring the board carries out its financial, legal and regulatory obligations. The four areas are explained in some detail in the Institute of Directors' (1995) *Standards for the Board*. These are not meant to be prescriptive: they are a guide to be used as a checklist or starting point. It is useful to see the activities as the board's annual review cycle. We have slightly adapted Bob Garrett's useful 'Simple Learning Board Model' (Garrett, 1996) to show how these activities work together to form a natural board cycle (see Figure 7).

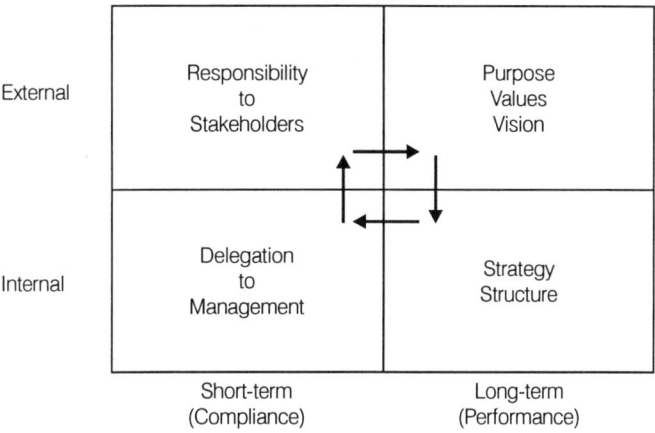

Figure 7 The cycle of board activities

Purpose, Vision and Values

We have already discussed the board's role in agreeing and articulating the organizational purpose, vision and values as a critical aspect of setting the direction for the business. It is a useful process for the board to revisit the purpose, values and vision each year. Are they still relevant? Is the business aligned to them? Are we acting in a way consistent with our purpose and values? Is the vision still useful; does it need changing? As part of the process of checking the relevance of the existing vision, an extensive audit of the external environment is important. The board then formally assures itself that it is aware of industry, market and other environmental changes that may affect the business. Annual external auditing is important for spotting emerging trends, identifying major opportunities and threats and for ensuring that the organization does not extrapolate from the picture the year before.

In addition, the organization's managerial objectives and policies need to be reviewed to ensure they are consistent with the purpose, values and vision. Companies can fall into the trap of having vision and values statements that bear little resemblance to the reality of what people in the organization are actually doing.

Where an organization's vision, for instance, is about becoming a leaner, flatter meritocracy, remuneration policies where the only way to achieve a salary rise is through promotion are clearly going to be dysfunctional.

Strategy and Structure

Strategy refers to the planned process for achieving the vision. It is the logic or rationalization of the steps that need to be taken. The board is responsible for strategic thinking but not for planning. The board's job is to generate all the possible routes to the vision – the strategic options – and to choose the options that will best achieve the vision, ensuring they are in line with the overall purpose. The board then delegates the planning of exactly how the strategies should be implemented to managers. People throughout the organization need to be involved in delivering strategy. Once the framework has been set by the board, it is a managerial responsibility to convert it into a series of implementable steps that are 'owned' by the people who have to do them. This is the best way to ensure that strategic plans are not documents that gather dust on a shelf while we get on with the business, but become guidance notes to be thumbed through every day. We have known one company where the Development Directorate acted as the 'guardians' of the strategic plan. The attitude was that no one should interfere or alter it, let alone develop it. Rather than a living document, it was treated as a holy relic!

Boards, and companies generally, are good at business planning but often leave strategic planning to a graduate or consultant, if it is done at all. The time horizon of strategy is longer than business planning. Business planning is an essential management task, culminating in the budgeting process, but will degenerate into extrapolations on previous years if there is no strategic framework.

Strategic thinking takes time and judgement. It starts with evaluation of the likely opportunities and threats that are arising from the external environment. The implications of these then need to be assessed. Some companies find it useful to build possible scenarios to try to picture what future changes might look like and the possible ways that the organization might respond. What is essential is that the board does not pay lip-service to the process, viewing it as an academic exercise with little relevance for what they are actually going to do. This implies closed thinking and predetermination of strategic direction which may prove to be inappropriate.

Some companies decide their strategy and persist with it even when environmental changes render it inappropriate. This occurs when the board goes from the tactical to the strategic rather than evolving tactics from strategy. The board needs to examine the external information as objectively as possible. We remember an occasion in one company when one of the future scenarios put forward was that the next government would be Labour. One of the directors insisted the scenario was abandoned, claiming it was provocative and speculative, mainly because it made him uncomfortable because the ramifications for the company were potentially significant.

Once the external analysis has been done, the board should objectively assess the organization's strengths and weaknesses. What needs to be assessed is the fit between the market environment and the organization. The clue to strategy comes from where there are misalignments between the two within the context of the vision.

Many directors find the process of generating strategic options pointless and frustrating. They often feel that the route the company must take is 'obvious'. This is symptomatic of not asking the question *why*; fundamental in strategic thinking. If the board has decided 'we need to do this', by asking the question 'Why?' it may be possible to find a different way of 'doing this' which is better, cheaper or more inventive. Another reason why generating strategic options is a crucial aspect of strategic thinking is because it is then possible to assess the risks associated. One route might seem 'obvious' at first sight but, when compared with others, might prove to be more costly.

Once the board has derived that strategic framework the next step is to assess whether the organizational structure is appropriate. Many of the blocks to strategy implementation lie in dysfunctional structures. This might then be extended to looking at an organization's capabilities and skills base. Do we have employees skilled in the new technologies we wish to utilize?

Delegation to Management

To help to ensure that strategy is implemented, the board needs to ensure that appropriate performance targets are set. It also needs to set targets to monitor that the company meets its legal and fiduciary responsibilities. The board must also satisfy itself that the internal control systems provide valid, reliable and relevant information for monitoring the company's performance.

The board delegates authority for implementing strategy, plans and policies to managers and then monitors progress, taking corrective action where necessary. It is not the board's role to become involved in operational management although the reality is that this is very common. As Garrett (1996) says:

> Unless the board chairman handles the supervision of management by the directors carefully, this is the black hole into which all the board's energies can be sucked, never to reappear (p 103).

The trouble is that many directors are more comfortable doing managerial activities. This is where they achieved their first major successes and they tend to repeat the behaviours that earned them rewards. They also tend to get involved because the information that the board receives is inadequate for making a clear assessment of what is going on in the business. This is what lies at the heart of the Cadbury Report: the need for boards to have a better grasp of the financial state of the company.

Part of the board's duty to management is to appraise and reward senior managers as well as disciplining incompetent managers. In addition, the board should ensure that managers are receiving appropriate training or personal development. Succession planning is something rarely seriously undertaken by boards but is an important element of ensuring the organization's long-term success. This means evaluating senior managers and selecting those with directorial potential for development into the role. Most newly appointed directors have received little, if any, preparation for the job. This is a theme to which we will return.

Responsibilities to Stakeholders

As stewards of the company the board of directors must ensure that it carries out its legal, ethical, fiduciary, financial and regulatory duties. This involves assessing its accountability to shareholders, suppliers, customers, the government, regulatory authorities, employees, the environment and the local and wider community. The company's relationship with each group should be monitored and nurtured. The company's level and quality of communication with stakeholder groups might also be evaluated. Close relationships with stakeholders help the board to establish each group's expectations of the organization. These can then be taken into account as part of the strategy process. To complete the loop, the board needs to communicate the organization's strategy to the stakeholder groups, partly out of duty and partly to show that their interests have been taken into account.

THE BOARD AS A PERFORMING TEAM

All members of the board, regardless of position, are equally responsible in law for the governance of the company. They share the collective responsibility for ensuring its successful long-term performance. They need to operate as a performing team. In our experience, however, very few boards act as teams. We know of a few that have acted as a team for a short time when united behind a short-term goal such as a management buy-out. But we do not see boards where members are recruited to complement each other, where collective responsibility is understood and where time is spent on individual and team development. As we have shown in this chapter, the role of the board is changing. If boards continue to work in conventional ways, they will find it increasingly difficult to respond to the new pressures. Most of us have been a member of a great team at one time in our lives, whether inside or outside the workplace. We know the levels of trust, commitment and energy that can emerge and the size of the mountains that can be climbed. Boards need to operate in this way to perform their complex role.

Working as a team means that directors must understand their roles – the different 'hats' that they need to wear. A board is not working effectively if the directors are acting in their capacity of heads of functions and competing with each other. This creates win/lose scenarios which are unhelpful for the overall organization and likely to be repeated right the way down through the organization. When operating together as a board, the directors need to look at the business as an integral whole. They need to create 'win/win' scenarios with employees and stakeholders. In the next chapter we will examine the individual director's role in more depth.

References

Capital Strategies (1997) *The UK Employee Ownership Index* as quoted in the *Financial Times*, 28 April 1997.

Collins, J C and Porras, J I (1996) 'Building Your Company's Vision', *Harvard Business Review*, Vol 74 No. 5, September-October

Financial Times (1997), 24 April, an interview with Gary Hamel

Financial Times (1997) 6 May

Financial Times (1997) 12 May

Garrett, B (1996) *The Fish Rots From the Head*, HarperCollinsBusiness, London

Harvey-Jones, J (1988) *Making it Happen – Reflections on Leadership*, Fontana/Collins, Glasgow

Hurst, D K (1995) *Crisis and Renewal – Meeting the Challenge of Organizational Change*, Harvard Business School Press, Boston MA

Institute of Directors (1995) *Good Practice for Directors – Standards for the Board*, IoD in association with Henley Management College, London

Kotter, J P (1996) *Leading Change*, Harvard Business School Press, Boston, MA

Pearn, M (1997) *Managers Making Mistakes: Moving from Blame Cultures to Gain Cultures*, Croner, Kingston upon Thames

Robert, C (1994) 'What do we want to create?', in Senge *et al.* (1994) *The Fifth Discipline Fieldbook*, Nicholas Brearley, London

Roberts, C (1994) 'What you can expect . . . as you build shared vision', in Senge, P *et al.* (1994) *Fifth Discipline Fieldbook*, Nicholas Brearley, London

UK Business & The Environment Trends Survey (1997), Moffat Associates Partnership, London quoted in the *Financial Times*, 15 April 1997.

Chapter 3

The changing role of the director

Learning to fly

THE JUGGLER OF HATS?

The company director has a complex job which is becoming more demanding. His first duty is to the company. He is legally responsible for the affairs of the company equally with all the other directors. In addition, he could be personally liable if found to be in breach of his duties. The members of the company, the shareholders, appoint the directors to govern the company on their behalf. They expect the directors to prevent failure and to ensure success by skilful analysis of the changing business environment. The role of director is a professional one. It requires a high level of skill, knowledge and personal integrity. A performing board requires each director to be contributing to the full extent of their capabilities. Directors are under constant scrutiny from employees inside and from stakeholders outside the organization, who all look to the directors to set the direction, values and standards.

Given the difficulty of the role and the potential personal risks involved, it is surprising that so many senior managers aspire to become directors. They do so largely because of the prevailing, but outdated, view of the position as a comfortable, powerful job with privileges that comes as a reward for years of successful endeavour as a manager. This perception, coupled with a lack of induction for newly appointed directors has served to perpetuate the myth. Many directors are finding themselves ill-prepared for the challenges of the role. They often feel an increased sense of responsibility but translate this into the need to know in even more detail what is going on. In this way, they act as super managers of their particular function or operational area believing that their role on the board is to 'defend their patch'.

Yet, becoming an effective director actually requires a change of attitude and approach. It means learning to direct instead of being a manager. Functional expertise becomes secondary to strategic thinking. In fact, approaching the job of company director from the point of view of a particular function such as marketing or production can hamper the ability of the director to contribute effectively to the board. Directors need to develop helicopter vision: the ability to see 'the big picture' and the part that their function does or should play within the whole. They have to learn to interchange between a number of potentially conflicting roles: director of the company, head of a function, manager of staff and role model for employees. Identifying these different roles and understanding which to assume and when is a critical first step towards becoming a director. Some directors have other roles, or 'hats' to wear. These include that of shareholder in the case of a management buy-out and manager of the board in the case of the chairman.

The pressures on directors are making the crucial task of managing compliance and performance more difficult. There is shareholder and public pressure on directors to improve standards of corporate governance on the one hand while on the other, rapidly changing market and environmental conditions mean that corporate renewal requires inspired leadership. Most directors we know are intuitively aware that their role has changed and that it now demands more than they have or are currently giving. Unfortunately, they tend not to invest in themselves to acquire the new skills and knowledge needed to support this until a crisis occurs.

The qualities that will make the outstanding director of the twenty-first century will be radically different from those of the past. The qualities of strategic thinking, leadership, listening and learning will supersede the traditional qualities of technical expertise, years of experience and the ability to make decisions. The director of tomorrow believes passionately in the vision for his organization and acts as a role model for others. He respects and supports his fellow directors but does not necessarily always agree with them. He is committed to his task of ensuring the successful future of the organization. His dreams are those of the organization. He pursues them even though they may bring no personal reward: he does it because 'it is the right thing to do'.

PERCEPTIONS OF THE DIRECTOR'S ROLE

Observing directors in action reveals that they believe their role is to manage the business. Many may know intellectually that they should be directing and delegating the authority for managing, but still tend to behave as 'super' managers nevertheless. As Garrett (1996) puts it:

> They have an understandable, but not forgivable, inclination to find any excuse to intervene in the managerial system as soon as they see a crisis

occurring, or to create a crisis themselves so that they can continue to demonstrate their managerial prowess (p 9).

Becoming a director is seen as having made it to the top of the organizational hierarchy. It is the reward for being ambitious and having performed successfully as a manager. The newly appointed director generally thinks that the job is to do what he was doing before but with greater responsibility and, therefore, power. He also feels the increased ownership for ensuring the future survival of the organization, although may translate this into demanding more control of his function to ensure that nothing goes wrong. In return, the director expects the perks that come with the most senior position in the company: respect from colleagues and employees, a lucrative salary, larger office and so on. He also expects to make decisions and not to be challenged or questionned; after all, he must know best otherwise he would not have been appointed.

You may think that we have painted a rather cynical picture of a group of people who make an enormous contribution to the success of our business organizations. This would be true when considering the conscious motivations of directors. Most are acutely aware of their responsibilities to the organization and work extremely hard to ensure success. Nevertheless, they generally channel their energies into managerial or tactical tasks. As a result of the increase in work due to board activities, such as board meetings, many directors 'disappear' from view and become unapproachable. This means that they can become isolated, lonely and out of touch with what is actually happening within the organization. Why is it that directors generally still behave in this way?

- The old style of directorial behaviour has worked successfully in the past. As we have said before, nothing breeds complacency as much as past success.
- Newly appointed directors look to existing directors to be their role models. In the absence of any other information, they will behave in the way they see other directors behaving around them.
- There is enormous pressure on new directors to conform and 'fit in' with the rest of the board. To achieve inclusion may mean they must behave in a way that ensures they are one of the group rather than in the way they think is right.

The changing role of the director

- Very few newly appointed directors receive any training or induction for their new role. This reinforces the pervasive attitude that the directorial role is merely an extension of what was done before.
- Many directors are more comfortable being a manager and are anxious that their function should continue to perform well because its performance reflects on them.
- More to the point, many directors are unaware of the need to change their behaviour or learn new skills. Those that are, may feel that they do not wish to have to start learning all over again or they do not know where to begin.
- Many directors feel that people in the organization expect them to have the answers so it would set a bad example if directors were to show any weakness and admit that they had anything to learn. They may also feel that it would be a sign of weakness and uncertainty to those who appointed them in the first place.
- There is little guidance as to what directors need to be doing, how they need to behave and what skills they need to acquire.

Employees also conspire to maintain directors' conventional ways of thinking and behaving. Managers think of their director as 'the boss': the person who has the ultimate responsibility if anything goes wrong. Managers expect their directors to know what they are doing and have all the answers. The directors are responsible for ensuring that the company has a future and for attracting new business. Managers expect support, encouragement and feedback from their directors. At the same time managers can often resent directors for creating too much bureaucracy, for interfering and for receiving all the glory when they do the work. Directors are expected to protect the employees and the company from the demands of external parties such as shareholders and the media. Employees will examine the directors' words and actions in the search for information about the culture and future direction of the organization: what is the acceptable way to behave in the company; which behaviours are rewarded, which are punished?

The reporting requirements of the board can be a source of frustration for managers particularly if they feel the information is being used to 'check up' on them. Communication from the board of directors is often poor. Managers then try to fill the vacuum by interpreting what they think the organization's strategy is, based on the few clues available. Very often boards and senior managers assume that everyone else knows what is happening and why, even though they have not communicated anything. Pieces of information that have come from an informal conversation that a director has had with a manager become extrapolated and used as guidance. The meetings that take place at board level are used to interpret what issues are of prime importance. The way directors respond to reports or other information they request from the management can be used to gauge where the focus of activity should be; people tend to do what you inspect rather than what you expect. Directors' secretaries become powerful people within the organization selecting, either with guidance or on their own initiative, who can have access to the board members and when.

In many of the organizations that we see, the board of directors acts as a constraint to organizational change. Directors, who as managers were among the advocates for change, suddenly become risk averse, blocking change initiatives. This is primarily because of the increased personal risk felt by directors. They know that 'the buck stops here' and the wrong decision could cost them their jobs. It was not long ago that middle managers were accused of being the block to organizational change. The picture we see now is quite different. Middle managers have adapted as a result of the recent years of redundancies, loss of job security and enforced personal change through rationalization. In client organizations today, we are more likely to see middle and senior managers frustrated by the lack of strategic direction coming from the board. They can see the necessary changes that the organization needs to make and are 'champing at the bit'.

There is a conspiracy, then, within our organizations to keep directors doing what they have always done. One of our clients (John Spencer of GTRM) produced the lists in Figure 8 which illustrate the point.

THE NEW ROLE OF THE DIRECTOR

It is time that directors seized the initiative for change and organizational development from senior managers. The public debate about standards of corporate governance in our organizations demands that directors fundamentally reassess the way they add

The changing role of the director

What do senior managers think directors do?	**What do senior managers actually see directors doing?**
• Deal with strategic matters and political issues. • Keep the shareholders at bay. • Control the bottom line of the company. • Keep an eye on the market, look for opportunities, develop the business and monitor its performance. • Have confidence in the senior managers who report to them and not see them as threats. • Communicate at high levels with clients. • Communicate at high levels with competitors. • Communicate at high levels with suppliers. • Direct in the broadest terms, leaving the detail to others. • Act as a buffer for the company. • Sip G&Ts, drive big cars and watch their share options grow! • Solve problems. • Take a long-term view. • Have high expectations. • Lead by example. • Command respect.	• Get involved in too much detail. • Manage rather than direct. • Make detailed decisions from too great a distance. • Not communicating effectively. • Not sharing the hidden agenda. • Being run ragged by the MD and shareholders in producing reports, explanations and papers – none of which is delegated! • Deliberately distancing themselves. • Seeing senior managers as threats to themselves. • Firefighting rather than planning. • Offering the Rolls Royce to clients but only providing the internal budget for a motorbike and expecting to see a Rover 600 with air conditioning!

Figure 8 A senior manager's perception of the director's role

value to their organization. In many cases, we would say that directors have so far been lucky to be able to persist with conventional practices. But this is now an issue of corporate governance. By not adapting, directors are preventing boards from performing in the manner required for long-term organizational survival. Rather than being risk averse by not changing, directors are enacting a high risk strategy because everything around them is changing: 'if you always do what you always did, you will always get what you always got'.

When thinking about their new role, a good starting point for directors is to understand the difference between directing and managing and then to stop managing. This will create the time and mental space to start the job of directing. Directing is all about leadership. The directors set the vision for the future direction of the organization and the strategy for ensuring the vision is achieved. Managers then implement the strategy using plans and budgets as tools. The directors communicate the vision to all employees through words and actions in order to align the organization's energy behind turning the vision into reality. Managers then organise employees so that their energies are channelled in a constructive and useful way. The directors set the example: they motivate and inspire in order to facilitate the best out of employees and the organization. Managers control and problem solve: they identify problems and manage the resources to solve them.

Learning how to stop being a manager is extremely difficult for directors. They have to stop doing something that they are good at in favour of something they are learning about while being observed by employees and external parties. They also have to learn to trust their successor within the function or operational area. There is a sudden shift from control and certainty to ambiguity and uncertainty. But the director is not alone. When the board of directors operates as a team synergy results and more is achieved than by the directors acting as individuals. Working collectively as a team also provides mutual support and a sense of purpose. This can give new directors the support they need to 'let go of the side of the pool and start swimming alone'.

Directors might find it useful to think of themselves as operating from the centre of the organization, rather than the top of the pyramid. They are the 'business brain (a term used by Garrett, 1996): the part of the organization that analyses information from inside and outside. It is also where thinking takes place. The emphasis then is on being acutely aware of external market forces and the organization's situation within the environmental context. Thinking strategically means seeing the company from many different angles. It also means thinking beyond the company and the industry to wider business issues such as considering the factors affecting customers' industries. Being the business brain does not mean that directors have the monopoly on good ideas. What is more useful is to act as the organizational centre for ideas from anyone including customers, suppliers and others. It includes building scenarios of what might happen in the future. Recently a director told us about the scenarios his company constructed before the recent election for how the company would work with a future UK government. They called the scenario 'The Blue Book'.

The changing role of the director

Once it became clear that a Labour government was likely to be elected, the board started to write 'The Red Book'. The scenarios were not perfect but at least the company was not taken completely by surprise. The time spent on this activity was, therefore, a good investment of energy and resource.

As we have seen, the Cadbury Committee was set up in response to public concern about the financial aspects of corporate governance. Its report highlighted the importance of effective auditing and internal control systems. Directors have the difficult task of thinking strategically at the same time as keeping an eye on the operational detail. This requires the ability to sift quickly through reams of detail and spot anomalies or trends. It also means developing the crucial skill of asking the penetrating questions: the ones that keep management focused, helping to spot potential crises before they happen. All this has to be achieved without the director allowing himself to become sucked back into operational management. One way to achieve this is by setting, communicating and reviewing corporate level performance measures and ensuring that managers cascade these down throughout the organization in the form of local performance indicators. As a professional who could be made personally liable for being in breach of his duties, it is imperative that the director is insured to protect himself, as are other professionals such as accountants, solicitors and consultants.

Directors significantly underestimate their ability to influence others through what they say and do. This should be used to build relationships both inside and outside the organization and to inspire staff to want to remain with the company and customers to want to do business. By changing their leadership style from command and control to facilitating and coaching, directors can help to provide a supportive and learning environment where people feel empowered. The aim is for employees at the sharp end to feel sufficiently supported and valued to generate their own answers to organizational problems and ideas for change on the basis that they know better than anyone else how to do it better, quicker or cheaper. Other ways that directors can engender a supportive environment include being approachable; by walking about rather than being confined to an office; communicating honestly and often to set an example for others to follow; and by publicly recognizing the contribution of staff at all levels of the company.

Learning to fly

Directors need to measure their own performance in order to measure their level of learning and effectiveness. Directors should also be careful how they reward themselves. Rewards must be linked with achievement against organizational objectives and directors need to be sensitive to the timing and communication of directors' rewards. Large bonuses at the same time as poor company performance is likely to be criticized by employees and shareholders, even if the rewards are justifiable. By communicating their personal performance against predetermined targets, directors will improve their accountability. Remuneration and rewards for directors must be viewed within the context of total employee rewards. Large discrepancies between average directors' salaries and average employees' salaries are not conducive to encouraging employee loyalty and commitment.

We believe this is the model for the future role of the director which will ensure that boards perform and lead their organizations. Some directors may already be acting in this way, some may find it easy to change their style. We believe that the majority of directors will find the transition difficult and will need help. This should come from the chairman and managing director or chief executive in the form of support for appropriate and ongoing personal development to develop new skills, thinking styles and behaviours. A crucial element of this ongoing personal development is an induction process to get new directors up and running as quickly as possible.

To achieve the transition in directorial role, directors will also need to manage the expectations of others. The nature of relationships will need to change, particularly with people in their functional area. By explaining exactly what his role is, the director will help people to change their expectations of him. If in the past people in his functional area were used to asking the director to solve all the technical problems or the major customer complaints, he will need to explain that this is no longer his role and ensure that his successor fills the gap. When we change, particularly if the change is rapid, we can leave family and colleagues confused. Since we are the ones that have changed, it is for us to explain what is happening and to allow people the time to understand the change.

Directors can also help to challenge preconceptions by setting an example in terms of how they balance their lives. The 'macho' style of management, synonymous with organizations that are overmanaged and underled, is unhelpful for directors who are learning to lead. Taking a more holistic appoach to organizational life can help to improve learning and performance even if, at first, it seems to be the 'softer' option. Creating a better balance between personal and working life, generating more thinking time and taking time out for learning are all ways that can help the director perform his role. To begin with, the director may need guidance in achieving this balance. He is surrounded by pressure to conform to a norm of behaviour which may no longer be appropriate but is nevertheless dominant. Breaking the mould is personally risky and isolating. There is often no one around to assure you that you are doing 'the right thing'. Coaching can be particularly useful in helping the director to feel less isolated by offering a sounding board, encouragement and experience from other organizations.

DIFFERENT ROLES ON THE BOARD

While anyone called a director is equally accountable for the affairs of the company, some directors will have different specific roles. The nature of these roles is changing. In particular, the Cadbury Committee recommendation that has been most widely implemented has been the separation of the roles of chairman and chief executive. In many companies traditionally one person has carried out these two different, and potentially conflicting, roles. The Cadbury Committee also recommended a number of changes to the role of non-executive directors to increase their influence on boards.

The Chairman

Contrary to popular belief, the chaiman is not the chairman of the company. He is legally the chairman of the board of directors. He is appointed by the directors who determine the exact nature of his duties. His main responsibility is to lead and manage the board of directors. He is responsible for:

> the working of the board, for its balance of membership subject to board and shareholders' approval, for ensuring that all relevant issues are on the agenda,

and for ensuring that all directors, executive and non-executive alike, are enabled and encouraged to play their full part in its activities (Report of the Commitee, 1992, p 21).

Any director can call a board meeting and the whole board share the collective responsibility of ensuring the board works as an effective team. But it is generally the chairman who enacts these duties. Managing the board comprises determining its composition, responsibilities, how it will be structured and how to improve its effectiveness. It also includes planning and running board meetings.

1. *Responsibilities of the board* – These need to be defined and communicated. This includes specifying the responsibilities that have been delegated to particular directors, especially the chairman and chief executive, to management and to board sub-committees.
2. *Board composition and structure* - For the board to function effectively its membership and organization must be determined and reviewed. This includes the selection, development and induction of directors; identifying omissions or overlaps in directorial roles; and organizing the board sub-committees.
3. *Planning and running board meetings* – This involves determining meeting schedules, agendas and reporting procedures. All attendees of board meetings must have some notice and receive sufficient information for them to be adequately prepared. The agendas for board meetings have to strike a balance between long-term strategic issues and short-term operational issues, such as reviewing budgets. Minutes should be taken as a record of the decisions and actions taken. They should also capture any dissensions. While there is no legal requirement for minutes, they can be the only source of evidence of board conduct, particularly if directors are subject to legal action.
4. *Improving board effectiveness* – This is concerned with ensuring that the board learns and develops. It involves setting and reviewing board performance targets; identifying strengths and weaknesses of individual directors where the performance of the board is affected, and team development. It includes the assessment of directors' decision-making abilities; their interpersonal relationships; and their attitudes in areas such as risk, change and ethical issues.

The chairman has a crucial role to play in ensuring that the board comprises a team of people whose individual qualities balance each other. Consequently he must take a lead in the selection and appointment of directors; in ensuring that new directors receive some form of induction; and for ensuring that individual directors develop the required skills, knowledge and attributes. Furthermore, he should ensure that the organization has a process for identifying and developing the directors of the future from the management team. We will discuss the development of directors in more detail in Chapter 5.

It is the chairman's responsibility as the head of the board to ensure that the directors are performing effectively: that they contribute fully as people with collective responsibility for the organization. This particularly applies to their legal, financial and fiduciary duties. One of the most important functions that a chairman performs is to provide balance on the board. Boards of directors are not usually comprised of individuals with complementary skills. They are more often dominated by a certain, usually powerful, type of individual. We have a tendency to recruit in our own likeness from type of personality to social background. This can lead to a lack of diversity of views, shunning of people and ideas that are different and a lack of critical judgement. It tends to reinforce a particular viewpoint and restrict a wider, more inclusive one. How many companies are now led by ex-financial directors whose main weapon is to cut costs and people? This is sometimes appropriate but is it to the extent that we see it today? If the only tool we have is a hammer we will tend to treat everything as if it is a nail. The chairman can act to encourage open debate, challenge preconceptions and bring in new directors with different views to broaden the perspective of the board. He may also need to identify and remove directors who are unsuitable.

The Chief Executive/Managing Director

While the chairman's job is to manage the board, the chief executive's role is to run the business. The chief executive is responsible for implementing the company's strategies and plans and for achieving the required results. In this way, the board delegates much of its power and authority to the chief executive to ensure that its vision is realized. This is why it is important that the roles of chief executive and chairman are separate. The position of chief executive is a powerful one and, if the board is not to become unbalanced with too much operational focus, it requires a strong chairman. In fact, especially in smaller companies, it can be helpful for the chairman to be a non-executive director. The board must monitor the performance of the chief executive carefully to ensure that he is using the power delegated to him appropriately. If necessary it can remove him from his position.

The role of chief executive is the most potentially powerful but also the most difficult role to achieve successfully. As the head of the company, management and employees, in charge of the company's day-to-day activities, it is difficult for the chief executive to avoid being the supreme manager. He must ensure that he retains his strategic focus and delegates operational matters to his team of executive directors. The role can be very isolating. The chief executive is usually expected to have all the answers and to make the difficult decisions. He needs to be clear, and to make sure that his fellow directors are clear, that the future of the company does not rest entirely in his hands but is a shared responsibility of all the directors. The chief executive is a 'first among equals'. One of our clients, the managing director of a sportswear company, recently made the point that when a board is truly performing and collective responsibility is really shared, there should be no reason why the role of chief executive should not rotate among the executive directors. This could be particularly useful in a rapidly changing company where different leadership styles are required for short periods of time. Such a concept brings the added benefit of consistency because all the directors will have agreed and be working towards the same long-term vision for the company.

Executive Directors

Executive directors are full-time employees of the company. They usually report to the chief executive but as directors are equally legally responsible for the affairs of the company. They must, therefore, be able to challenge the chief executive and other members of the board and participate fully in issues related to the whole company, not just their area. Executive directors are usually responsible for enacting company plans and ensuring results in a functional or operational area, such as production or marketing. This usually reflects their area of expertise and experience. The executive director, therefore, must learn to alternate between wearing his operational hat and his directorial hat. Ultimately he is a director of the company and must see his functional responsibilities within that context. Rather than looking at the company from a marketing department point of view, the marketing director must assess what his department should do in order to fulfil its role in meeting overall company objectives. By taking this strategic approach, directors can avoid the 'turf warfare' that can take place between functions competing for scarce company resources.

In fact, it is essential that all directors publicly support and respect each other if the board is to fulfil its leadership role. This tone of mutual respect and acting within a strategic context means that disputes and disagreements can be channelled positively to help the board learn. It also means that executive directors will sometimes have to make hard decisions about their functional area in the short term for the long-term benefit of the company. The executive director is not there to defend his area but to use his knowledge and expertise to decide how the company's strategies should be applied within the area and to inspire his employees. For a new executive director who has been promoted from a senior managerial position, this is a difficult change of style and approach. It is very easy to be a director in name alone and continue to act as a manager. This attitude leads to inter-functional conflicts at board level which permeate throughout the organization. In companies where R&D do not talk to Marketing, for instance, the root of the dissension may lie at board level. It also leads to executive directors not fully participating in board activities. They tend to concern themselves only with matters relating to their functional area; for instance, by defending their function's performance and being uninterested in the performance of other areas except where there might be a conflict of interest. Executive directors owe it to themselves and their company to remember at all times that their first legal responsibility is to the company.

Non-Executive Directors

Sometimes referred to as independent directors, non-executive directors are part-time members of the board. They are not employees of the company and do not have any functional responsibility. Nevertheless, they have the same legal responsibilities as any other director on the board. The main role of the non-executive director is to bring an impartial external point of view to the workings of the board. There is no legal requirement for companies to appoint non-executive directors. However, there is great advantage to be gained by their effective presence. The Cadbury Committee's report states that non-executive directors have two crucial roles to play in improving standards of corporate governance. First, to review the performance of the executive and the board as a whole and second, to take action where conflicts of interest arise. The latter is particularly important in corporate governance terms because the interests of the executive directors may at times conflict with the company's interests. The Committee's Code of Practice, which is obligatory for listed companies, states that:

> The board should include non-executive directors of sufficient calibre and number for their views to carry significant weight in the board's decisions.

and that:

> Non-executive directors should bring an independent judgement to bear on issues of strategy, performance, resources, including key appointments, and standards of conduct (Report of the Committee, 1992, p. 58).

The Cadbury Committee recommended that there should be a minimum of three non-executive directors on a board. Their selection and appointment should be a formal process and a matter for the whole board. They should only be appointed for specific terms because their independence could be compromised by serving for too long. To ensure their independence from the company, non-executive directors should be paid an agreed and published fee which recognizes their contribution without seeming to compromise their independence.

The Committee went on to recommend more specific ways that non-executive directors should contribute to the workings of the board. A cornerstone of the report was the recommendation that boards should set up an audit committee constituted entirely of non-executive directors:

The changing role of the director

> A separate audit committee enables a board to delegate to a sub-committee a thorough and detailed review of audit matters, it enables the non-executive directors to contribute an independent judgement and play a positive role in an area for which they are particularly fitted, and it offers the auditors a direct link with the non-executive directors (Report of the Committee, 1992, p. 29).

It was also suggested that non-executive directors should play a role in the selection and appointment of directors. It suggested the setting up of a nomination committee, comprised largely of non-executive directors, to propose new appointments to the board. Finally, the Cadbury Committee suggested the setting up of remuneration committees as a sub-committee of the board; a recommendation that was expanded by the Greenbury Committee Report on Directors' Remuneration. The remuneration committee should, again, consist of non-executive directors and should be responsible for proposing executive directors' remuneration to the board. An essential element of this is that non-executives are then responsible for assessing the executive directors' performance.

The Cadbury recommendations on the role of non-executive directors drew some criticism. Sir Owen Green, Chairman of BTR, pointed out that '90 per cent of all recent corporate failures will have had non-executive directors on their boards' (Clutterbuck and Waine, 1994, p 5). The point is that the effectiveness of non-executive directors depends on the goodwill of the executive directors. Traditionally, non-executive directors have been appointed for their contacts or to bring credibility to the company. They were not necessarily expected or allowed to contribute to the running of the business. This partly helps to explain why the non-executive directors were not able to prevent some of the recent corporate failures. The executive directors must respect and see the value that the non-executive directors can contribute. They must review the information supplied to non-executive directors to ensure that it is adequate to allow them to make a full contribution to board matters. If the executive directors perceive the non-executive directors as a threat or a nuisance, preventing them from getting on with the job of running the company, then the non-executive director's role becomes extremely difficult. If, however, the executive directors welcome an objective insight into the company and their performance, then the non-executive director has a valuable role to play.

The non-executive directors must monitor their own performance. One of the main reasons for ineffectiveness is the reluc-

Learning to fly

tance to ask the right questions. This might be through fear of 'making waves' or of hostility from other board members. But this is a major part of the non-executive director's role. He must recognize that he has a right to information, to ask questions that challenge preconceived thinking and to express concern. Knowing how and when to intervene is a skill that has to be developed:

> It is difficult to say which is worse: the independent director who has little to say on anything, or the person who can not prevent himself or herself from offering an opinion on everything (Clutterbuck and Waine, 1994, p117).

Non-executive directors' performance should be assessed in the same way as executive directors' performance in the sense that each is a member of a team with different roles but a common objective. One method is for an independent third party to assess performance and feed back to each director on a one-to-one basis.

So, the greatest value that the non-executive director can offer a company is the fact that he is not '... trapped into the attitudes, values and short-term objectives of the executive team' (Clutterbuck and Waine, 1994, p 3). Apart from their participation in board sub-committees, non-executive directors can make a number of other contributions:

- they can challenge introverted thinking by asking the intelligently naïve questions;
- they bring experience from other organizations;
- they can offer specialist knowledge or an international perspective, particularly to smaller companies;
- they can help to balance the composition of the board, such as by providing different personality types or women;
- they can provide access to the non-executive directors' network and are often more comfortable dealing with third parties, such as government departments, than the executive directors;
- they can provide support to the chief executive and the chairman who may become isolated;
- they can offer moral and ethical guidance.

Sir John Harvey-Jones has suggested five key non-executive roles (Clutterbuck and Waine, 1994, p 29):

1. *the emperor's clothes* – having the confidence to ask naïve questions;
2. *the oil can* – lubricating relationships;
3. *Bank of England* – bringing famous name respectability;
4. *father confessor* – the wise confidant;
5. *high sheriff* – riding into town to get rid of the chairman or other directors.

The chairman of a company will normally appoint non-executive directors. Selecting the right people is not easy. Using the position to reward loyal, long-serving employees is a mistake which conveys a misunderstanding of the role. Unfortunately, many non-executive directors, especially of large companies, are trawled from the same pool. While they bring experience, these directors must begin to lose some of their objectivity. Unfortunately the typical non-executive director has his own *status quo* that he wishes to preserve – a sort of gentleman's club, if you like – and they also tend to be over 50 years old. The risk for companies is that older non-executive directors may be stuck in this traditional role and not know the relevant current questions to ask. The reason for appointing non-executive directors in the first place is to gain fresh insight and an external point of view. This suggests looking outside the traditional pool of non-executive directors and looking for younger people. It is important, when selecting non-executive directors, to balance experience with a fresh perspective and to ensure the individuals selected complement the other members of the board.

KNOWLEDGE, ATTRIBUTES AND BEHAVIOURS

What are the personal qualities that a director needs to contribute effectively to a performing board? To begin with the director must possess a certain level of knowledge which he must ensure he updates regularly. It is essential, for instance, that he has a full appreciation of his legal, ethical, fiduciary and financial responsibilities since, in law, ignorance is no defence. The director should also ensure he has a full understanding of the workings of the board and any guidelines pertaining to this, such as Codes of Best Practice. He should also be familiar with the current thinking on management and business practice. In terms of knowledge about the company, the director must be familiar with the Memorandum and Articles of Association. He must know the company's strengths and weaknesses, its strategies and vision in detail as well as the company's environmental context. This includes having an appreciation of the political, social and economic environment both in a wide sense and in terms of the company's position within it.

Below we list the personal qualities that directors need to have or to develop if they are to perform effectively in their role. It is probably unreasonable to expect every director to possess such qualities but it is essential that the board as a whole has all the qualities represented. The directors' skills and personalities should ideally be complementary. A board comprising all innovative and creative individuals will realize very few of the ideas generated. Similarly a board dominated by strong operationally biased directors will spend insufficient time thinking creatively about strategy. Focusing on developing the following qualities will help directors to define their role.

Strategic Thinking

Thinking strategically is something that is relatively easy to describe but difficult to do especially when inside a company looking inwards. The essence of thinking strategically is developing the ability to step mentally outside the organization and look at it from a number of different angles. It means being able to see where the organization sits within its market environment and to assess how that environment is changing over time. This includes knowledge of customers' and shareholders' environments too which leads to an appreciation of their motivations. These are clues to the strategic direction that the organization needs to take. Thinking strategically is having the ability to assess objectively the organization's strengths and weaknesses and to visualize the impact that various different actions might have upon them.

Thinking strategically means stepping back from the immediate problem in order to see the underlying issues as well as being able to see how disparate issues actually link together. It is like fitting the pieces of the jigsaw together in order to see the picture rather than trying to see it from a few pieces of the puzzle. Operational crises do not become all-consuming because they are seen in the broader context. Crisis management is also more effective as it is possible to assess the long-term consequences of short-term actions.

People who think strategically are able to think along time horizons. They do not just live in the present but are able to see how the organization has developed in the past and picture how it will look in the future. They can create a vision of the organization's future. This allows them to be comfortable with change because they can picture what the long-term effects of change will be. Strategic thinkers are generally creative and innovative in their approach to organizational change but also have the ability to bring judgement to bear. They can, therefore, generate many options and then choose the most suitable idea for the success of the organization. Good ideas only become good strategies when they become practical, realistic and realizable. Really skilled strategic thinkers are able to articulate their visions because they can see from different perspectives. They can explain how different people or different parts of the organization will be affected by strategic change. They are also able to evaluate operational plans in terms of whether collectively they will ensure the company meets its strategic objectives. When others get lost in the operational detail, the strategic thinker asks, 'will this action achieve the long-term strategy?' They see tasks and actions as steps on a mental journey towards a future destination; and because they know where they are going, they are able to be flexible about how the journey is undertaken as long as the overall direction remains the same.

Commercial Focus

Developing commercial acumen is an extremely useful skill for directors because it can be used to evaluate ideas and decisions quickly and simply. Will implementing this idea benefit our customers and make the company more money? People who have developed an innate commercial focus subconsciously evaluate everything that the company does in this way. They also have the ability to look at potential ideas and actions from a customer's perspective. Developing commercial acumen can save the director time and effort. It can also help him to be more decisive. An apparently excellent and logical suggestion can be rejected because there will be no benefit to customers.

In our experience, this sort of thinking is especially useful for evaluating changes in organizational structure. By asking, 'How will customers benefit from our internal structural change?' the director can ensure that organizational resources are not wasted on changes that realistically amount to little more than moving the furniture around. Commercial acumen is also critically important for evaluating new product ideas because it brings the crucial element of objectivity. The sudden realization that a product is not right can be a hard decision to reach. If it can be seen from the point of view of customers, not only is the decision easier to take, but it is possible to work out how the product needs to be changed. Lack of commercial focus can cause companies to make disastrous mistakes. Some 90 per cent of new products launched on to the market will fail.

Communication and Interpersonal Skills

Many directors find that their position means that people can be in awe of them. They become unapproachable to the average employee. The director must develop the ability and confidence to communicate at all levels of the organization. He must also be confident and competent at communicating with all external interest groups whether a customer who has a complaint, the media or a trade union representative. The director who successfully masters communication and interpersonal skills tends to view the organization as patterns of human interactions rather than as things. He has realized that business is about relationships and that the better the relationships work, the better the organization will work. He generally works collaboratively, aiming for a 'win/win' outcome from every encounter. Great communicators leave people inspired and feeling better after the interaction than they did before. As leaders, directors must be able to communicate the company's vision in a way that galvanizes employees' energies. They also recognize that communication is more than words. They make themselves visible and approachable; they behave congruently so that their actions reflect their words and they spend more time communicating than in any other activity.

The excellent communicator has learned to listen. In this way he can develop rapport with his audience and convey his message in a way that they can relate to. This ability to listen can have enormous benefits when handling difficult interactions. During a change programme the director will know that an important part of achieving success will be allowing the time and attention to listen to employees. There is a tendency for boards to want to implement change programmes quickly because then the pain will be over and life can get back to normal. This often means that insufficient time is given for people to move through the change process and the programme ultimately fails. By listening carefully, directors can assess when to move on from one stage of a programme to another. Directors who interact with potentially hostile external groups can be far more successful at diffusing that hostility if they listen and develop rapport. This prevents a defensive response which may escalate such problem encounters. Part of developing as a communicator is the director understanding that it is impossible to over-communicate. This means having a passion for the vision which is conveyed to others in everything that the director says and does.

Example 6

A board of directors with which we have worked was about to launch a communications programme to explain a new vision. Most of the directors were not comfortable presenters and so formal speeches and slide packages were prepared to ensure that the message conveyed was consistent. At the start of a series of major presentations to employees, the chief executive began by following his script. At the end of the first presentation he was frustrated because he knew he had not convinced his audience. At the second presentation, he stood at the rostrum and visibly put the script to one side. He used no notes or slides but spoke with passion for about half an hour about his personal vision. He was so graphic that his audience were left convinced and excited about the future, even if they did not appreciate the intricate details of the changes. When people talked about the vision it was often referred to as the chief executive's vision.

Analytical and Detail Conscious

For directors to perform their compliance obligations effectively they must be skilled at analysing data. They need to be able to spot trends or anomalies from masses of information. They also need to know which information is relevant and which is potentially 'muddying the water'. There is a difficult balance to be struck between getting submerged in detail and retaining a strategic focus. However, directors must not be tempted to delegate all of their reporting authority to managers as they will lose their route to finding out exactly what is going on in the organization. Skilled analytical thinking combined with a strategic focus will ensure that directors can find the important trends or spot the potential crises. In addition, it means that they know the state of the company in detail and can speak about it with authority at any time.

Results Oriented

Directors need to be able to make things happen if they are to achieve the required level of organizational change. By being results oriented, directors can prevent the common organizational malaise of activity without purpose. Directors who are achievement driven tend to set high standards for themselves and have high expectations of others. They show great determination in spite of obstacles and problems. They are able to retain their levels of energy and are persistent even when it looks as if everything is against them. Above all, they are resilient and tenacious. They are able to remain effective, composed and focused even in the face of overwhelming criticism and opposition. They may feel anxious or under stress but do not allow it to be seen, to affect their judgement or to deter them from their objective.

Team Player

Collective responsibility requires directors to become team players. Having collective responsibility means that everyone works for the good of the organization and has a shared vision. This comes above directors' individual aspirations. Being a team player means that the directors have recognized that more can be achieved by working as a team than by working as a group of disparate individuals. However, becoming a team requires determination, commitment and a change of behaviour. Board members need to learn to be open in order that they can be trusted and, in turn, learn to trust others. In the highly competitive world of the senior executive, becoming a team player requires a leap of faith. However, it is a leap worth making. Creativity, energy and effectiveness will all be increased as anyone who has been involved in a performing team can confirm. Boards deal with complex problems where there is no single right answer. Finding the best option for solving the problem requires the sort of thinking that cannot be provided by a single individual or a group. It requires the added value that team working can produce where people combine their talents to achieve an exceptional outcome.

It is beneficial for directors to become team players as they are not so isolated but can support each other through periods of great uncertainty. It also means that they have accepted that they do not have all the answers or all the skills necessary themselves. They need their colleagues so that the board can perform collectively.

The result of learning and acquiring new skills and knowledge will be that directors will feel equipped and confident to change their behaviour. Figure 9 shows the shift in behaviour that is required.

Old – 20th century	New – 21st century
Independent	Team player
Champion of function/area	Sees how function fits in big picture
Knowledge is power	Knowledge is to be shared
Has the answers	Asks the right questions
Isolated	Communicator
Prefers certainty	Comfortable with ambiguity
'Super' manager	Leader
Tells	Listens
Decisive	Facilitates others to make decisions
Maintains the *status quo*	Challenges the *status quo*
Holds meetings	Develops relationships
Talks	Thinks
Can be found in his office	Walks about
Is the boss	Is a role model
Seeks agreement	Allows loyal opposition
Competitive – I win/you lose	Collaborative – I win/you win
Advises	Coaches

Figure 9 The director's new role requires new behaviours

Learning to fly

But how do we create the space to allow directors to demonstrate and practise the behaviours that are essential for the twenty-first century? These new behaviours are alien for most organizations and the pressure for directors to behave to the existing norm is huge. The starting point is to break down some of the traditional structures and conventions that typify the current role of the director. We suggest below some simple steps that you can take to help create the organizational environment where the new directorial behaviours can be explored.

STEPS TO HELP DEVELOP NEW DIRECTORIAL BEHAVIOURS

1. What is in a name? In the case of the director, a great deal. We suggest that one way to dismantle preconceptions about the director's role and to encourage directors to move from the mindset of their particular function, is for all members of the board simply to be called 'director'. Thus, rather than A being the Director of Marketing and B being the Director of Production, they are both just called Director. This does not affect their functional responsibilities but will send a message to the rest of the organization (and themselves) that their primary responsibility is to direct the organization.
2. Taking this a stage further, we also suggest that the functional responsibilities of the executive directors on the board are rotated at regular intervals. So, the manufacturing director might take over as sales director for a short term of, say, six months. There are a number of advantages to such an approach:
   — because the director is unfamiliar with the detail of the function, he is able to ask the intelligently naïve questions which challenge and encourage new thinking;
   — he is less likely to interfere in the managerial decision making of the function;
   — it encourages cross-function understanding, breaking down traditional organizational barriers or empires;
   — the director is able to see his function from the viewpoint of another;
   — it helps the director to develop a picture of the whole organization and its interactions.

3. We have talked of the need to develop mutually beneficial relationships with stakeholders. One way to encourage this is to initiate 'one-to-one marking' of directors and stakeholders. Thus, a director might be given a customer, supplier, regulator and shareholder with whom he must develop a close working relationship. He would be responsible for ensuring that his 'partners' are informed of the company's activities and strategies and for feeding back their views to the board.
4. Seek out an independent wise counsel or coach to help each director to keep the focus on developing new behaviours, as it is all too easy to slip back into more familiar and comfortable patterns.
5. Get together with boards from other companies to exchange views and learning.
6. As a board generate a list of the behaviours that you wish to develop and regularly check whether they are being demonstrated.
7. Identify which directors already demonstrate one or more of the needed behaviours and use them as a model. For instance, if a director is recognized as a good communicator it would be useful to ascertain exactly what it is that makes him a good communicator. What does he do? What are his beliefs? How might others learn from him?

We have shown that the role of the director in our organizations is changing. Many directors have yet to respond and change what they are doing so that it meets the requirements demanded by today's boards. We believe that for personal and corporate survival directors must start to acquire new knowledge, skills and behaviours which allow them to perform as effective boards responsible for corporate renewal. Above all, the new style will enable them to become leaders, a subject that we address in the next chapter.

References

Clutterbuck, D and Waine, P (1994) *The Independent Board Director*, McGraw-Hill Book Company, London

Garrett, B (1996) *The Fish Rots From the Head*, HarperCollinsBusiness, London

Learning to fly

Report of the Committee (1992) *The Financial Aspects of Corporate Governance*, 1 December, Gee and Co Ltd, London

Chapter 4

New perspectives on leadership

THE ESSENCE OF THE ROLE OF THE DIRECTOR IS LEADERSHIP

What are the elements of good leadership? We tend to know intuitively when someone is a good leader but often find it difficult to articulate exactly why. Our belief is that there is a leadership vacuum in many of our organizations. The focus in the recent past in academic and business circles has been on improving management, with leadership receiving scant attention. This trend is changing as more people come to recognize that good management alone is not enough and that to be world class organizations need good leadership. Neither should leadership be seen as a substitute for management: the two are complementary. The first providing the vision, energy and direction and the second turning the vision into reality.

Traditional, well-established notions of leadership have their roots in western society's individualistic psychology and rotate around people who have strong, dynamic personalities and make significant or controversial decisions, typified by the heroic figure or charismatic leader. Fundamental to this model of leadership is the assumption of the powerlessness of the majority of people. We believe that this traditional model of leadership is inappropriate for today's organizations.

The new model of leadership is values- rather than task-based. New leaders set the context or environment that fosters the energy, enthusiasm and sense of shared purpose that is needed for organizations to achieve ongoing change. They are the custodians and articulators of the organization's vision. New leaders have rewritten the implicit contract that exists between them and other organizational members from one where leaders order and workers do to one based on mutual trust, benefit and responsibility. They create the environment in which other people can succeed. Their behaviour sets the model of how others should behave in the new organizational era. Their conviction dictates the level of commitment required by other members of the organization to the vision. New leaders have the rare and special capacity of being able to show how everything and everyone fits into the bigger picture. These leaders create a tension, a gap between the vision and current reality, and energize their organizations to bridge that gap. New leaders have a passionate, rather than possessive, belief in the vision which inspires others to become involved in its realization.

People who exemplify the model of leadership just outlined are not necessarily born. They have made themselves that way through a lifetime of developing conceptual and communications skills, reflecting on personal values and aligning their behaviour with these values, while learning how to listen and appreciate others and their ideas.

In other words, contrary to popular belief that there are only natural leaders, it is possible to learn how to become a successful leader of today. Fundamental to this process of learning is a change of attitude. Leadership is not a job: it is a role, a way of behaving and being. It is about behaving in a way that others wish to emulate.

If the picture that we are painting of today's leaders shows similarities with our earlier description of the new role of the director, this is no coincidence. Directors should be the leaders of their organizations. Ultimately this is what distinguishes them from senior managers and one of the reasons they should have the title director. They are there to direct the business; to lead it to future success. The essence of the role of the director is leadership. Learning the critical elements of leadership must, then, be a top priority for the developing director. He must recognize that he is expected to be a leader and that the nature of leadership in organizations is changing. Moreover, he must recognize that he is a member of the organization's leadership team – the board. Leadership is less and less about the great, charismatic individual. The task is too large and complex now for one person alone. The board has collective responsibility for leadership. It is the leadership team.

DEFINING LEADERSHIP

The term leadership means different things to different people, as can be seen from the quotes from some of our clients. It underlines the fact that the definition of good leadership lies mainly in the hands of those being led.

Learning to fly

> **What does it mean to be a leader?**
>
> 'The ability to face up to difficult decisions, to assess a situation from all its angles. The ability to delegate, to earn respect, to motivate, to give the impression that you would "do it" too.' (Ray Sale, Managing Director, CIA Media Solutions)
>
> 'I believe the essence of it is understanding what your people want you to be. The rest is dressing. You can put on a show, but that's all method.' (Ray Bush, senior manager, London Underground)
>
> 'First, to have a vision about what you're doing. Second, to be scrupulously fair and even-handed. Third, not to change direction but to stick by it because you lose credibility if you back off something and fourth, to be a people person…to be respected by the people you employ and be visible to them.' (Tony Smith, Managing Director, First Engineering)
>
> 'It can be different things in different environments and I think we have to adapt to the climate we're in, in terms of what is expected of a good leader. Leadership for a young organization might have to be much more hands-on and directive. Once the organization matures you can be much more participative in the way you do things.' (Primrose McLaughlin, Human Resources Director, First Engineering)

Leadership is about people: it is the process by which they are influenced to behave in a particular way or to do particular things. This is what distinguishes it from management which is primarily about tasks; problem solving and resource allocation.

> Leadership is a set of processes that creates organizations in the first place or adapts them to significantly changing circumstances. Leadership defines what the future should look like, aligns people with that vision, and inspires them to make it happen despite the obstacles (Kotter, 1996, p 25).

Leadership is about change, influence and persuasion.

The recent overemphasis on management has meant that people within organizations have been treated as any other organizational resource or asset. Yet, organizations are fundamentally networks of

New perspectives on leadership

relationships between people, with success being determined by how well they interact and improve their individual performance. To a large extent this depends on how well they are led. Treating people as an organizational asset, rather than the heart and soul of the organization is, we believe, a fundamental error made by many organizations. How many times have we heard or read the phrase, 'people are our greatest asset'? It is a cliché. More importantly it reflects how people in organizations are treated by their 'leaders'. Yes, people might be the greatest asset, but more importantly they are individuals with energies, ideas and emotions that, when harnessed, can produce outstanding organizational performance.

Organizations that have difficulty changing and adapting more often than not lack leadership. The dominance of management leads to inward-focused bureaucratic cultures that stifle creativity and learning. Without leadership to inspire and generate internal energy, change initiatives have to be pushed and are rarely successful.

Why is it that leading people seems to have disappeared from our organizations? One reason is that managers are more comfortable dealing with tasks and tangible things than with people. Moreover, many businesses have enjoyed enormous success as a result. The rationalization and 'rightsizing' strategies of many companies in the recent past emphasize the management approach where people in organizations were as expendable as any other business asset or overhead. Such an approach shows a fundamental disregard for people and their worth. It also reflects the absence of leadership.

It is relatively easy to make large numbers of people redundant in troubled times but it does not address the underlying business problems that caused the crisis in the first place. People hold the key to solving such fundamental problems providing they are properly directed. This is not to say that we believe organizations should never make people redundant. That would be unrealistic. But we do believe that it should be a last resort and that people, themselves, should have the right to make such a decision. We have witnessed some successful delayering programmes where people, faced with the realities of a changing business, accepted voluntary redundancy or early voluntary retirement rather than face the pain and uncertainty of change. The point is that organizations have been able to perform relatively successfully without providing leadership for their people.

A second reason why leadership has disappeared from our companies is that the traditional styles of leadership no longer fit the organizational context. Leaders in the traditional style tend to base their authority on their technical competence, hierarchical position or charismatic personality. The emphasis of the traditional leader is on having all the answers, making all the decisions and telling people what to do. By implication, such leaders need to have complete knowledge bordering on omnipotence which is increasingly unlikely in today's business world. In telling people what to do they stifle opposition and creativity. Even the charismatic leader cannot rely on sheer force of personality alone. What is important for enduring success is to be able to convert that charisma or power into energy for the business. Well-known charismatic leaders of today, such as Richard Branson and Alan Sugar, remain effective because they have learned to share their leadership role internally.

Are Leaders Born or Made?

There is a widely-held view that leadership is really all about personality and that either you have what it takes or you do not. Traditional concepts of a leader revolve around extrovert, self-confident and highly competent individuals. In fact, many of the most successful leaders have tended towards introversion, such as Bill Gates, but they have personal qualities that inspire others to follow.

Personality, we would argue, is just one aspect of leadership. Leadership has three components:

1. *the leadership task* – setting the goal or direction, communicating and motivating others towards the goal;
2. *the leadership qualities* – such as personal integrity, understanding of people and communication which inspire others to follow;
3. *the leadership style* – how the leader goes about the leadership task and using the leadership qualities.

The first two components of leadership can be learned and will improve and develop over time. The last point is to do with personality. As one of our clients put it:

> The style, I believe, is to do with your own personality. *How* you do it is down to are you this type of person or that type of person? And the style will influence the rate of progress that you make or if you make any progress at all.

This managing director went on to explain that achieving the other components of leadership was like 'taking yourself out of your own body...'. In other words, these are the elements of leadership that must be adapted to suit the environment and the people being led at the time. Successful leaders have the ability to assess the environment and pick the most appropriate leadership approach for the time which may or may not fit with their personality. There will be occasions, therefore, when leaders will have to make a conscious effort to repress certain personality traits which are inappropriate or develop new ones. Effective leadership relies on the effective *use* of personality rather than on personality itself.

Do Leaders Have a Shelf-life?

We have said that the leadership task and personal qualities can be learned and that successful leaders will adapt their style to suit the business environment. The implication of this is that leaders need not have a shelf-life. In practice, however, they tend to. Why should this be so? The business environment is moving so quickly that there will be occasions when the leader's approach does not adapt quickly enough. George Davis, the creator of the Next retail chain, was hugely successful at first but did not adapt his approach to suit the rapidly changing retail sector so the business went into decline for a while until he was replaced.

Some leaders become 'stuck' in their particular style because it has been extremely successful and they are reluctant to change a winning formula. Margaret Thatcher's command and control approach was successful during her early years in power but became less effective as the country moved out of recession. This reluctance to disturb a successful leadership formula is very common and reflects a reluctance to learn on the part of the leader. They are usually isolated from feedback about their performance, either because people will not openly challenge them or because they see criticism as a personal attack possibly motivated by jealousy. The leader's ability to adapt and learn is helped considerably by the presence of a trusted, objective person who can help the leader see where he is going wrong and what he needs to do to put it right.

Some leaders develop an approach, partly based on their personalities, which suit businesses in a certain mode, such as in crisis. Leaders who become particularly proficient may be sought after by companies when they are in that mode. For instance, David James was brought in by the ailing Sears retail group to retrieve something from the loss-making British Shoe Corporation. James has a reputation for rescuing companies in serious financial difficulty, often in the face of overwhelming hostility from existing management and employees.

> ### Case 5 – Patrick Gillam
> Patrick Gillam has recently been appointed chairman of Royal & Sun Alliance. He has gained a reputation in the City for achieving business turnarounds. Up until 1991, he had spent his whole working life with British Petroleum and only left when he realized he 'wasn't going to get the top job, and I didn't want to retire at 60'. Since then he has been chairman of Asda and Standard Chartered and is attributed with hauling both organizations out of a serious financial mess. Mr Gillam believes his success has been the result of choosing the right businesses: 'If you want to try to concern yourself with reviving and restoring companies, you had better be sure that the industry you are in is one which is capable of reviving'. He is an example of a leader who has developed a style to suit businesses which require rescuing and deliberately seeks leadership positions that match his preferred approach.

THE CHALLENGE OF LEADERSHIP TODAY

As we stressed in Chapter 2, if organizations are to survive and prosper in today's competitive environment they must continually change and renew themselves. The role of the leader is to ensure ongoing business transformation by motivating people to do adaptive work (a term used by Heifetz and Laurie, 1997); this is when fundamental changes in organizational behaviour are required which challenge previous values or norms and where what was once successful is no longer appropriate. 'Adaptive problems are often systemic problems with no ready answers' (Heifetz and

Laurie, 1997, p 124). The challenge for leaders is to realize that such problems are not technical challenges for which they must have the solution. Rather the leader's task is to tell the organization that they do not have the answers but that the organization must collectively find the best possible approach to the problem. To achieve this leaders have to learn to ask difficult questions, challenge existing thinking and stop protecting the organization from market realities. For the leader who has achieved his position of power as a result of his technical ability and experience as well as his ability to give 'solutions', this new leadership approach can be a shock. Above all, it means that the leader's power comes not from technical competence, experience or position, but from his ability to persuade, influence and communicate his sense of vision or purpose in such a way that it motivates others.

A fundamental leadership task is the creation and articulation of an organizational vision. In today's organization, this is not something that any one leader can devise by himself; it is unlikely that he will have the answer. His job is to see the 'big picture' in order to see the context for change, such as a new market trend or consumer pattern. Alternatively, he must create the context for change by, for instance, persistently facing employees with potential problems to generate a sense of urgency for change. This is an area where leadership is quite distinct from, but complementary to, management. Being able to see the organization and its environment from above – as if from a helicopter – is not easy. Avoiding the temptation to get sucked into the scene that you are trying to observe is difficult and a critical test for the leader. But for organizations to successfully achieve their visions they need leaders who are able not only to maintain their focus on the vision but can ensure that everyone else in the organization maintains focus as well. Leaders must generate and maintain shared visions.

The leaders of today are change agents. They know that if the organization stands still it will die. They take the responsibility on their shoulders, often unasked and unrewarded, for ensuring that change happens. They do this because they know it to be the right thing to do. They have conviction with which they are able to 'infect' other members of the organization, thus establishing a collective sense of responsibility for the future. This can be an enormously difficult, lonely and risky task. Leaders must have high personal commitment.

Learning to fly

More than just being change agents, leaders must also understand the dynamics of change and the effect it has on people. Major organizational change can be distressing because it can be threatening, requires new behaviours and challenges existing certainties. In the past employees would look to senior managers for reassurance and to minimize their distress. They would expect the leader to protect them from reality. However, rather than protecting people from the realities of change, new leaders need to protect them by managing the rate of change. People can only learn and adapt as fast as the slowest essential person in the organization. Impatience on the part of the leader is likely only to increase stress and the chance of failure. Thus, leadership is about balancing the need for people to change and the rate at which that change takes place.

> To use the analogy of a pressure cooker, a leader needs to regulate the pressure by turning up the heat while also allowing some steam to escape. If the pressure exceeds the cooker's capacity, the cooker can blow up. However, nothing cooks without some heat (Heifetz and Laurie, 1997, p 127).

Achieving this dynamic tension means seeing conflict as a way of finding the issues rather than something that needs to be quelled. At the same time, however, it means setting the change context for people so they are not thrown into panic by the lack of structure. This might be achieved by converting the new business realities into different roles and responsibilities, for example.

Treading the knife-edge of creative tension that is organizational change puts the leader under great personal pressure. He will not be immune to the pain, frustrations and distress that change generates. In addition, his every action and word will be scrutinized by all members of the organization, as well as interested parties outside, who will be constantly checking that the leader remains on course. Any slight hint of uncertainty on the part of the leader will be taken as an excuse to take the foot off the accelerator by the rest of the organization. Leaders must, therefore, be resilient and able to keep their nerve when all around them are losing theirs.

Is it any wonder that leadership is lacking in our organizations when its realization is so difficult? Yet the leader need not be alone. In fact, he owes it to himself and to the success of the organization to surround himself with people whom he can trust, who will give him a true but constructive picture of his performance and who can give him emotional as well as practical support. This is where his peers and a coach can be invaluable.

The other, potentially huge, area of support for the leader comes from the organization's employees. Unfortunately, many employees have become used to a patriarchal style of management. This means that senior managers have prided themselves on making the difficult decisions and protecting employees from responsibility. This has led to passivity and habitual work patterns and a reluctance to take responsibility. The leader must overturn this pattern of behaviour. First they must persuade managers to share the responsibility for decision making with all employees. Second, they need to encourage self-belief and self-confidence among employees. How can it be that people can hold responsible positions within their local communities, such as being a school governor or parish councillor, and be unable to make simple decisions at work without referring them to a senior manager? This is partly a result of habit and partly because of a fear of making a wrong decision. Instilling confidence, therefore, means encouraging people to take personal risks and not blaming them for mistakes.

Encouraging people to take responsibility for the organization is extremely difficult. How often have you heard phrases like, 'that's not my job' or 'I don't get paid enough to do that'? Generating collective responsibility means that people must recognize the problems faced by the organization, the likely effect of these problems on their area and be able to influence or enact a solution themselves. Instilling a sense of collective responsibility might be hard but the rewards are enormous. The energy generated by people whose collective energies are focused on a common goal can be amazing. If people believe it to be worthwhile, they will make an enormous personal commitment to an organization which will be visible in the amount of responsibility without authority that they are prepared to take on, the hours they are prepared to work and the risks that they will take.

This is what empowerment is actually all about. The word has become something of a cliché to suggest giving power to employees as well as a say in the future of the organization. But this is only half the story. In return, employees have to share in the responsibility for their part in the decision-making process and the organization's future. They need the guidance and support of the leader. More importantly, the leader needs to create a trusting environment. The employee who puts his head above the parapet only to have it shot at is unlikely to try it again. Saying that employees are empowered is easy; we read it in many annual reports. Making it happen is difficult. The leader has to offer protection to whistle-blowers; those individuals who can see potential problems and often find it difficult to articulate their concerns well. They also have to offer protection to the creative individuals who suggest ideas which completely challenge current thinking. Both sorts of people are traditionally crushed by organizations looking for homogeneity.

To create the environment where loyal opposition is tolerated and where debate is encouraged demands a change of leadership approach. It is about working towards collaboration – towards win/win outcomes and alignment. But it also means being tough when toughness is required. Sometimes leaders in search of collaboration get stuck in trying to be too consensus-seeking and risk becoming ineffective and 'wishy-washy'. They should not avoid making the hard decisions when necessary. The focus should be on trying to take others with them when taking the hard decisions.

Part of not having all the answers is that the leader has to encourage others in the organization to generate solutions. This requires a change of approach from 'tell and sell' to 'coach and listen'. Some years ago we conducted some research where we asked people to generate two lists; the first was the qualities that they would want to see in a leader and the second was the qualities they would want to see in a coach. Both lists turned out to be exactly the same.

Renegotiating the Leadership Contract

As we have already suggested, the leader's success depends greatly on how he fulfils the expectations of the people who follows him. 'The leader's position is best found in the hearts and minds of the followers' (Mileham and Spacie, 1996, p 21).

The leadership contract is the implicit contract that exists between leaders and followers. If the nature of leadership needs to change to reflect the changes taking place in business, then it follows that this implicit contract will also need to change. In many of today's organizations the implicit contract is based around followers doing the work and leaders taking the credit. From another perspective, leaders take all the risk and the blame if anything goes wrong and followers get to say 'I told you so'. Followers look to the leader to tell them what to do, to set an example and to make decisions. Leaders expect loyalty, commitment and unquestioning obedience from their followers.

In today's organizations such a contract is dysfunctional. Followers who have these expectations of their leaders are placing an unfair burden on the shoulders of the leader and opting out of taking any responsibility for the future of the organization. This is neither realistic nor tenable. It is clear in some organizations that employees are increasingly dissatisfied with this sort of relationship. They know that the leader cannot have all the answers; he is often too remote. They are 'champing at the bit', eager to take greater responsibility because they can see more clearly than the leader what needs to be done.

We see many examples of senior managers frustrated by the out-of-date implicit leadership contract that exists with their leaders, the board of directors. This reflects the more general change in the employer-employee contract. Employees have had to adapt to changing employment conditions. A job for life is no longer something that employers can guarantee. A decade of redundancies as the response to recession has taught employees that they need to rely less on employers to look after their interests and become more self-reliant. Employees whose skills are in demand ('career-fit employees' to use the current jargon) will rate a challenging job which helps their personal development more highly than job security or levels of pay.

Leaders, particularly at board level, are taking longer to come to terms with the fact that the leadership contract is changing than their employees. This is usually because:

> ...(they) have to break a long-standing behaviour pattern of their own: providing leadership in the form of solutions. This tendency is quite natural because many (directors) reach their positions of authority by virtue of their competence in taking responsibility and solving problems (Heifetz and Laurie, 1997, p 124).

Part of the reason that leaders find it difficult to change the implicit contract that exists is the fact that followers and the structure of the organization usually conspire to maintain the *status quo*. It is difficult, therefore, for leaders to develop the confidence to say to their followers 'I do not have all the answers but we, collectively, may'. The tendency on the part of leaders and followers is to see such a statement as 'passing the buck'. The work of the new leader is not as transparent and obvious as the old leader making all the decisions. Followers may not be consciously aware of the work the leader is doing to create the environment that allows them to be creative, that increases their effectiveness and allows them to take a greater lead in the future direction of the organization.

The leader, therefore, must begin the process of contract renegotiation by making what is implicit explicit. We would suggest that any new leader should have an open discussion with his followers to elicit each other's expectations; an expectations exchange. Once out in the open, the leader can make it clear what his followers can expect from him and suggest what he expects in return. This may require some debate since part of this process involves followers accepting an increase in responsibility for the overall group performance. An expectations exchange can be enormously useful for agreeing a new, more appropriate relationship between leaders and their followers. It can also ensure that neither party is disappointed by the other.

We often see groups frustrated by their leader because their expectations are not known and not met. Similarly, leaders often dismiss followers as being incompetent or ineffective because their expectations have not been met either. If all parties have agreed up-front what can be expected from each other, a more constructive and open relationship will be formed. It also allows for self and group assessment of performance because tangible criteria have been set against which leaders and followers can check regularly on performance.

The responsibility for making the implicit leadership contract explicit and renegotiating it belongs to the leader. He will find it helpful to remember that at some time or other we are all leaders and all followers. In other words, part of being a good leader is learning to be a good follower. We have seen many boardrooms composed of very strong individual 'leaders'. These directors are usually not good followers. At best they will accept decisions from the chairman or chief executive grudgingly and at worst they will ignore them and continue to 'do their own thing'. Some directors need to learn humility, respect for their leaders and how to be good followers. There seems to be a sense of losing face among directors when they have to take on the role of follower. In reality, they will have more influence in board decisions if they act in the interests of the board team and the company overall.

New perspectives on leadership

In Figure 10 we have summarized the basis for the new leadership contract: what followers can reasonably expect from their leaders and what leaders can expect from followers. We believe that by making these expectations explicit, leadership can find a place again in our organizations. The results of changing the leadership contract will include:

- less time spent on politics and criticism behind the scenes
- wider base for creative ideas and innovation
- greater commitment and lower staff turnover
- decrease in stress levels
- people have a voice and sense of responsibility.

Leaders	**Followers**
• share results	• are not 'yes' men
• have confidence	• do not rebelliously conform
• allow followers to do it their own way (except where safety critical)	• show loyal opposition when necessary – prepared to question
• use difference as a dynamic force	• abide by the final 'cabinet' decision
• know the secret is alignment not agreement	• volunteer ideas and suggestions
• allow loyal opposition	• show loyalty to leader – public support and collective responsibility
• listen to criticism and new ideas	• are honest
• know which are the good ideas	• have integrity – do not undermine leader's efforts
• put it all together and articulate it so others can buy-in	• are trustworthy
• are visionaries	• do not expect too much of the leader
• build trust	• share the blame for mistakes
• build and protect the team	• have a desire to learn
• build relationships and coach followers	• raise problems early
• are good followers	• are team players
• make a commitment	• can survive and make decisions without the leader when necessary
• recognize responsibility *with* rather than responsibility *over*	• share the leader's vision
• recognize innovation and ideas are not their responsibility alone	
• allow the team to take the glory	
• are loyal to their followers	
• make the tough decisions when necessary	
• recognize their jobs is to create the environment in which followers can succeed	

Figure 10 The leadership contract

Leadership Qualities

If you were to ask a number of people to list the personal qualities that leaders require the list produced would probably be very long. However, it is likely that there would be a number of qualities that would appear on all the lists. These are the core attributes or qualities that characterize good leadership. It is useful to emphasize these major qualities because they can be used as a checklist for the selection of leaders. The list of qualities can also be used as a guide for personal development for directors and other leaders. The point is that these qualities would appear to be the hallmark of good leadership behaviour and, we believe, can be learned or developed over time, if one is aware of them. In essence, leaders need a repertoire of influencing skills. We do not think that the list of core attributes is exhaustive. We have highlighted those that we feel to be most relevant for leadership today.

Communication

Leaders influence by communicating. Being able to communicate is, therefore, a prerequisite for aspiring leaders. Most communication in organizations is poor. More often than not, information is seen as a source of power and not shared. Leaders have to develop outstanding communication skills to be effective. It is probably not going too far to say that communicating will probably be the activity they do more than any other. In this way ideas and information are spread and a shared vision can be fostered. Unfortunately we know of more poor communicators than good ones. And even those who seem good can improve. In other words, all leaders should be acutely aware of how and when they communicate and how they can improve. Communication is two-way and one of the most difficult tasks for the leader is to learn how to listen. But listening can be enormously rewarding. For one thing the people who are being listened to feel valued and important; that what they say is of interest. Second, it is by listening that leaders will find the answers to the organization's problems. The collective innovative and problem-solving ability of people is colossal.

Congruence

Communication is not just the things we say. Communication is not something confined to briefings or presentations. It is there in every word and action. Everything the leader does has a message which will be interpreted by followers. This is why it is vital that the leader's words are matched by his actions and behaviours. If he says one thing but does another people are likely to believe him to be insincere. Really effective communicators are congruent. The key to congruence is being clear about, and committed to, an outcome.

> If parts of you are undecided about, resistant to, or uncommitted to your chosen endeavour, this incongruence will be apparent to others in your external behaviour. They might notice you shaking your head no, while your words say yes. Your voice may quaver when you say strong words...All of these behaviours confuse others and weaken your influence (Laborde, 1987, p 186).

Developing congruence means learning to notice your discomfort when communicating and trying to ascertain the cause. It also means that the organization's vision must become the leader's personal vision if he is to articulate it with sufficient passion to excite others in the organization to the same vision.

Understanding of People

As we said earlier, leadership is about people. It is fascinating to us that so many people in leadership positions can talk about leadership with almost no reference to people at all. Good leaders have a deep respect for, and an intuitive understanding of, people. They are curious about what makes people tick. They are intrigued by differences in people. They are not threatened by people who are different from themselves but seek to learn from them. They usually have an ability to see situations from other people's perspectives which helps them relate to many different types of individual. This ability also allows them to adapt their communication style to suit different audiences. To take this a step further, good leaders are also curious about themselves and want to learn from those around them. They are aware of their own weaknesses and seek people with complementary qualities; rather than surrounding themselves with people in their mirror image. They are also not afraid of criticism because they see it as an opportunity to learn about themselves and the person being critical.

Confidence

By confidence we do not wish to imply extraversion. What we mean by confidence is a self-assurance; a sureness about oneself and one's purpose. If a leader does not believe in himself, it is unreasonable for him to expect others to believe in him. With confidence comes other related qualities such as resilience and decisiveness. Confidence stems from a peace of mind about your purpose and mission. It means that you know you are doing the right thing which allows you to be resilient and persistent when those around you are being critical or losing faith. It also ensures that you are decisive when necessary because you do not doubt your long-term goal and your ability to get there.

Personal Integrity

Perhaps one of the most important leadership qualities of all. Leaders have a strong moral responsibility towards their followers to behave with decency, honesty and integrity because people in organizations will model their behaviour on that of the leader. Many of the examples of poor corporate governance that we looked at earlier come down to a lack of personal integrity on the part of directors. Robert Maxwell is, perhaps, a prime example. One way to test personal integrity is to assess whether the leader is committed and has taken personal responsibility. Does the leader feel ultimately responsible for the success of the business or is he likely to 'pass the buck' when things start to get difficult?

Different Leadership Styles

It is perhaps tempting to think that there is a leadership formula: a set of behaviours and tasks which will ensure success. Unfortunately, while there may be some common elements that can be identified about successful leadership, there is no such thing as the perfect leader or ideal leadership profile. Psychologists and management theorists have developed numerous leadership theories since the 1940s illustrating the elusive nature of the subject. The recent revival of interest in leadership has also spawned more theories and texts on the subject.

It is our observation that there are as many leadership styles as there are leaders because the final essential element of the leadership role is personality, and we are all different. Thus, each leader brings his own unique contribution to the role. This is also what makes leadership so essential within organizations. It is the human element. Management has become an increasingly scientific practice to the point, as we discussed earlier, where people are often seen as being the same as other physical organizational assets. This has to an extent dehumanized business in recent years. Leadership represents the excitement, the flair and the inspiration. Organizations that recognize the need for good leadership have come to understand that business is really about people, their interconnections, relationships, ideas and passions. They believe that harnessing people's energies is the key to outstanding, rather than mediocre, business performance.

Often when we think about the leaders we have known in our lives, who have inspired us and from whom we have learned, it can be quite a surprise. They may not be the romantic hero type of individual that we would expect. Who was the first person in your life (other than your parents) who really influenced you? Who was the first person in your business life who really influenced you? What was it about this individual that marked them out as a leader? By observing traits that we admire in other leaders who have influenced us we can improve our own leadership style. This is a useful exercise because when first asked why they think someone is a good leader, people will often reply, 'I don't know, there is just something about him'. On deeper reflection, however, and by closely observing behaviour, certain patterns and styles will emerge which can be modelled. It is much the same as examining any accomplished or skilled person. If you ask a great sports person, or a skilled typist or a musician how they do what they do, they will find it difficult to answer. They have developed a skill through practice to the point where it has become subconscious. This is what aspiring leaders are aiming to achieve.

Just like the musician who will interpret a piece of music in his own individual way, so leaders bring an individual aspect to their leading. We offer a number of examples of different leaders we have known or who are in the public eye to illustrate how radically

Learning to fly

different leadership styles can be and yet still be extremely effective. While there is a leadership task to be done, effective leaders will remain true to who they are.

> **Example 7**
>
> Examples of some leaders we have known are:
>
> - One director we know has enormous intellect and technical competence. He has become a director as a result of his technical knowledge for which he has earned great respect. The trouble is that he finds it difficult to let go of the detail. If there is a technical problem, he is happiest if he is in the middle trying to sort it out. His people management skills are generally from the command and control school. He believes that people who do not perform should be sacked rather than developed or trained. On the other hand, he believes that good people should be trained and developed to their full potential. Why waste money on people who will not make it anyway?
>
> Yet this individual commands huge loyalty from those who work for him to the extent that they follow him when he moves to other organizations. As one person put it, 'however bad, whatever he is, I know where I stand with him and he is fair'. Among the attributes that make him a leader whom others follow, is his openness to ideas and criticism. If someone disagrees with him, he does not dismiss them but hears what they have to say. He also recognizes that he needs to do things that he may not personally be good at but that need to happen. He has been instrumental in implementing a large-scale change programme within his functional area which is now recognized to be about two years ahead of the rest of the organization. He did this by gathering a team of people around him and providing them with the top-level cover that they needed to achieve the work. Another person who worked for this director described him as:
>
>> ...a great boss to work for. He became very interested in teams in principle, although I think naturally he was a great individualist. But with the passage of years he came to the view that the whole

is more than the sum of the parts and if you create a team then you get much more output than from disparate individuals.

Above all, he is very loyal to his people. People who have worked for him are more loyal to him than the organization that they work for, being prepared to follow him to whichever organization he moves to.

- By contrast, another director we have worked with believes in bringing feelings to work. The morale of his team is extremely important to him. He believes that by looking after people's morale, welfare and the things that are important to them as individuals, they will improve their contribution to the workplace.
- The chief executive of a large utility company was a leader who inspired thousands of workers. Everyone felt as if they knew him and called him by his first name in spite of the fact that they still often called most of their immediate superiors by their surname. This man had reached his position, as did most senior people in the organization, through technical competence. However, his leadership style was unique. Rather than adopting the style of the other directors around him which was generally directive, authoritarian and distant, his reflected his personality. He was demanding, easily irritated and found it virtually impossible to stay out of the detail. But he also possessed qualities that people followed, even if they had never met him in person. If he needed to know something quickly he would more than likely go and find the person he needed to talk to in their office rather than asking them to come to his. This was in marked contrast to the traditional habits of other directors in the organization. He also had a vision: a firm picture of what the organization was capable of achieving with a bit of effort. He had a passion for the industry and a belief in its future which was in contrast with the often cynical view of many of his colleagues. While at times this made him blind to some of the problems of the business, it also inspired a renewed pride in the organization. He would discuss his vision with whoever would listen. In an organization that was ferociously hierarchical, he was fundamentally egalitarian. An introvert by nature, he was also sociable, friendly and made himself approachable to everyone.

Learning to fly

As leader he initiated a major organizational restructuring, cost cutting and refocusing programme. He had to begin by persuading his fellow board members that this was a necessary action. This was not easy since the majority would see their 'empires' and their personal power considerably reduced as a result. Once he had his board behind him, he set about communicating the need for change both up and down the organization. He trusted his board and his team of change agents to plan and implement the details of the change. He saw his role as legitimizing the need for change and communicating it both inside and outside the organization. When the chief executive left a few years later, much of the organization was left shocked and depressed.

- A managing director we know of had a philosophy of 'giving his people so much head room that it would make them air sick'. He selected his people with great care but then left them to get on with the job. He was obsessive about time management, loyal to his people and took the blame (and credit!) for his people's actions. He sometimes made himself deliberately unavailable to force his team to solve their own problems. When they did turn to him for a decision, he would first of all coach the individual to solve the problem for themselves. He would then stand by that decision as if it were his own. This did not mean, however, that he did not make decisions when necessary. However, he saw his main task as developing his team. He was friendly and sociable but retained a distance from his team which helped to further their deep respect for him.

Case 6 – Julian Richer

Julian Richer is a young entrepreneur who established Richer Sounds, a hi-fi retail chain, in 1979. The business has been extremely successful as a result of Richer's innovative ideas and obsession with customer service. His business is in the *Guinness Book of Records* as the world's busiest retailer. He has become well-known for his unusual ideas with companies such as Asda, the Halifax and Sears all seeking his advice. His advice to Asda included advertising for recruits in *Viz* magazine, allowing the company Jaguar to be used by high-performing individuals, standing at meetings and a company suggestion scheme.

Richer's own company suggestion scheme is 'the king-pin of the organization, generating many of the new ideas that have been investigated' (Donkin, 1997). Richer believes in continuous improvement and knows that new ideas are the life-blood of his business. Employees are given £5 a month to go to the pub to discuss ideas. Customers are the dominating force in the company. Large portions of staff bonus payments are based on customer satisfaction targets rather than sales.

Richer is an entrepreneur with a unique leadership style. He has a relaxed and friendly manner, placing great importance on creating rapport with everyone, particularly new members of staff who spend their first few days with the company at a training centre at his home. Richer rewards good employee performance with, for instance, use of classic cars and holiday homes. But he is also demanding and controlling with an eye for detail. He is intolerant of dishonesty. Employees are instantly sacked for any form of theft. This has reduced 'shrinkage' in the Richer stores to around half the average for a retail store. In the case of Julian Richer, people seem to follow him because of his ideas, his success and his fairness.

Case 7 – Bill Gates

The chairman and co-founder of Microsoft, the world's largest computer software company, Bill Gates has been phenomenally successful. As a leader he is a visionary. He has the ability to communicate his vision in real and practical terms so that it is so familiar it becomes an inevitability. He recently committed his vision to paper in his best-selling book *The Road Ahead*. Another of his leadership hallmarks is his highly competitive nature, which, combined with his passion about his vision, gives him the confidence to take risks. Under his leadership Microsoft, now a huge multinational organiza-

Learning to fly

tion, still achieves response times that a small business would envy. It jumped on the bandwagon of digital television within days of the US Federal Communications Commission allocating channels to US broadcasters. Gates believes 'the migration to digital TV is a big opportunity for the PC'. His vision is that PCs will be capable of receiving digital signals and be very much cheaper than digital TVs.

Gates works extremely hard and focuses his efforts on communicating his vision to everyone, both inside and outside the organization. He makes frequent speeches and presentations as well as press interviews. He is passionate about ideas. As part of Microsoft's ongoing learning strategy, the company announced in June 1997 that it was setting up a major research group in Cambridge, UK. It has also set up a collaborative arrangement with Cambridge University whereby Microsoft will help to finance the University's science faculty and the University will share computer research staff in return. One of the reasons for his success is his tenacity and resilience. Microsoft have had a number of unsuccessful forays into the domestic PC market which Gates does not see as failures but as set-backs, 'Patience is a key element of success'.

Case 8 – Laurence Bossidy

After 34 years at General Electric, Laurence Bossidy took over as chairman of AlliedSignal six years ago. The company has since done well with its shares performing twice as well as the average on the USA stock market. Bossidy's leadership style might at first glance seem old-fashioned as he believes AlliedSignal's success is due to its focus on four processes: a people selection and training process; a strategic planning process; a budget process; and a customer satisfaction process. Yet on closer examination he exhibits a number of leadership qualities that have contributed to his, and the company's, success.

First, he has an ability to see the 'big picture' and, more importantly, the trends and patterns developing in the future. He takes a worldwide perspective and is able to see the past and the future in context.

He was quoted recently as saying:

> I'm convinced that in whatever way, the Germans will come back, and the French. We know the Japanese are going to come back. Certainly, the Chinese and the Indians are going to be major world competitors. So though things are good now in the United States, this is the time you lose it. We'd better tend to our knitting, or these days will change and change fast (Bossidy, 1997).

Bossidy believes that companies' and individuals' inability to see the wider perspective is a major reason for failure. He argues that many corporate failures are due to their introspection and isolation. He believes that organizations must learn from each other. He also believes that corporate development will not happen without personal learning:

> Never before in business have you had to invest so much time in becoming contemporary. Even if you sit at the same desk for the rest of your life, you'd better get a lot of new skills all the time (Bossidy, 1997).

Another major factor in his leadership style is that he understands that he is the leader. He does not get involved in management tasks and seeks to use his influence to motivate people.

> I don't participate in price decisions or factory scheduling. I am in no position to do that. You have to pick the things you can influence, and get out of the way for the rest. I can influence people because I know them (Bossidy, 1997).

TEAM LEADERSHIP

We have stated that leadership is the essence of the director's role. The director is there to lead rather than to manage. Yet he is also a member of a team that has the collective responsibility for leading the whole organization. Directors have to see themselves as leaders in their own right and as part of a leadership team. In this sense, they are also followers since the leadership team will, itself, have a leader. This individual should be the chairman, although in practice in many organizations it will be the chief executive or managing director.

The leadership task in organizations today is too important and too complex to be left to one individual. As we have shown, leadership requires a number of qualities or attributes which may not all be present in one individual but could be in a team. A team approach to leadership allows people to focus on their strengths. Often there will appear to be a single leader to the outside world because this is the person who is the skilled communicator and takes on the role of articulator of the vision. However, behind him will be someone who is a good strategist and helps determine what is said and where.

Boards of directors that see themselves as, and operate as, a leadership team will perform more successfully than boards that have one individual who has the leadership task. Team leadership gives boards the opportunity to realize the collective talents of all the directors which will achieve more than a single individual can. The issues that businesses face today are not simple technical problems. They are complex cross-functional issues that:

> require a deep expertise in specific areas, complemented by insight into the interrelationships between functions. Few, if any, individuals have the intelligence and breadth to deal with this kind of complexity on their own... (Kiefer, 1994, p 436).

Turning the board of directors into a leading team will not be an easy task for the chairman. The first problem is persuading a group of individual 'leaders' with strong views who are used to making solo decisions to co-operate with each other to generate collective decisions. The second problem is that, unlike most teams, there is no higher level authority that the team can turn to in the event of disagreement. Ultimately it will be the team leader, the chairman or chief executive, who is not impartial, who makes the final decision. Then the other directors must abide by and publicly support the decision. Third, the board of directors operates in an unforgiving environment. The leadership contract that we referred to earlier means that people in organizations still look to leaders for the solutions and protection. This makes them intolerant of mistakes, an inevitability when a group of people are learning how to behave in a different way. If the board of directors as individuals and as a group go into the process of learning how to lead fully cognizant of the pitfalls ahead, it should make the task less daunting. Finally, in order to get to board level people have normally had to be very competitive. Now they will need to change to become more collaborative and this will not be easy.

LEARNING TO LEAD

Developing leadership skills will not happen overnight. Directors need to view learning how to lead as individuals and teams as making a commitment to life-long learning. The first step is accepting that learning and personal change are required. This means a change of attitude. Directors have to understand that leadership is a role; a mantle or vocation, not just a job. They must be free of management. They need to let go consciously of everything they know and are comfortable with and look at old situations with new eyes. This is a great deal to ask of directors. It is made worse by the fact that boards generally have little support. We suggest that boards should not begin this learning process before putting some form of support structure in place. It is lonely at the top, as any managing director or chairman will agree. Members of boards need to be coached individually and collectively to help them maintain their learning focus and not to be deterred by setbacks. Equally, the members of boards should coach and support each other; after all you are all in this together. In the next few chapters we look at director development in more detail.

While we believe that learning to lead takes time, we also think that there are a number of actions that boards can take quickly to start the process. Leadership is an urgent requirement in most of our organizations and directors need to respond to the challenge immediately. Directors will need to learn how to lead on the job. Below we offer some practical suggestions. These are actions which boards can take to generate some 'quick wins', begin the learning process, and send leadership signals to the rest of the organization.

Learning to Lead – Action Plan
1. Renegotiate the leadership contract within the board of directors. This means having an open discussion with the head of

the board about the role of the leader and the role of the followers. The next step is for the directors to undertake the same process with the teams that they lead. This will set an example for others in the organization to follow.
2. Have an open debate at a board meeting on what leadership means for your organization. What are the obstacles to the board performing its leadership responsibilities? Do you collectively have the leadership qualities? The outcome of this might be a list of the board's leadership strengths and weaknesses which can be used as a benchmark for individual and team development and as a checklist for the selection of new directors.
3. Discuss the idea of rotating the role of leader so that the most appropriate nominal leader is chosen for different phases of the organization's life. This is a radical step for many organizations. A starting point from which to learn more about the concept could be to rotate the leadership of board discussions on critical issues. This would mean that directors would take 'ownership' for certain company-wide issues beyond their area of functional responsibilities. They would lead the board through the diagnosis of the problem through to a collective agreement about what to do and then implementation of the decision throughout the organization. Directors acting in this capacity should call themselves 'Leader of...(whatever the issue happens to be)' to send the message that their task is to lead the organization through the issue rather than try to solve it themselves.
4. All organizations, and particularly boards, communicate poorly. Learning how to communicate better begins with raising the awareness of the issue into consciousness. One way to do this is to conduct an honest assessment of what takes place currently. This should include verbal and non-verbal communication. Such a review will only have validity if it involves those the board are trying to communicate with, both internally and externally. The next step would be to agree collectively a formal communication programme for a specified time period. Without a structured approach, many boards are likely to plead *mea culpa* but actually do nothing different. It may be that some form of communications training is required. What is probably more essential is practice and cre-

ating opportunities to meet people. The most obvious message that the board needs to communicate both internally and externally is the organization's vision and this should be the starting point for any communications programme. It will be important to be honest about the board's attempts to improve its communications performance. You will not get it right first time. Ask your audiences for feedback. Feedback questionnaires at the end of presentations, seminars, meetings and so on can provide you with a great deal of information on how much of the message has been absorbed and how much more work needs to be done. It can also give feedback on communications and leadership style. Conducting question and answer sessions in small groups of up to 50 people can be an incredibly powerful way of learning how to lead. The leader is on the spot. He has to think on his feet and people will only believe what he says if he is consistent. It is also a way of visibly generating two-way communication; giving people a say in the debate. Finally, it is a method that makes the leader very visible and will help him learn to become more approachable.

5. Lead by example: this means doing as you say and recognizing that leadership is about being a role model. Be honest about inconsistencies (organizational incongruities) and correct them at the earliest opportunity. If the vision you are communicating is all about cost cutting to get the organization in shape for the future, then the board should not be spending money on lavish hotels for its strategy meetings. Rather it should set the example by, perhaps, not accepting the annual bonus.

6. Adopt a new approach with direct reports and ask for their help in so doing. Rather than telling them what to do, try to use a coaching style to encourage them to make their own decisions. As leader, your role is to set the context that allows them to act. Make time to see direct reports regularly on a one-to-one basis to talk about them as a person, rather than the job or the current task.

7. Be aware of, and develop, the behaviours which will help you learn to be a better leader including listening, soliciting the opinions of others, taking personal risks, self-reflection and being open to new ideas.

8. Leave people alone to get on with their jobs. Accept that there

may be some mistakes at first but trust people that they may do a better job than you give them credit for. Help them to see the context for the task, how it fits within the overall picture so that they can see the contribution they are making to the overall corporate vision.
9. Ensure that all members of the board speak and act as one. Regulate one another's behaviour and encourage loyal rather than disloyal opposition. This means having the courage to state up-front if you disagree with something rather than complaining about the decision at a later date. It also means abiding by collective decisions even if you would not have 'done it that way'.
10. Identify and appreciate the leadership qualities of your colleagues on the board. What can you learn from each one of them? What unique contribution does each make to the leadership team?
11. Demonstrate loyalty to people by accepting responsibility and assuming their mistakes as your own. Provide teams with space and protection to allow them to be as creative as possible.
12. In times of crisis, do not be tempted to compromise your personal integrity under stress. Persistently remind yourself and those around you of the overall goal for which the organization is aiming. This will help you to see the way through short-term crises, rather than getting sucked into them.

References

Bossidy, L (1997) quoted in an article by Tony Jackson in the *Financial Times*, 5 June

Donkin, R (1997) writing in the *Financial Times*, 27 March

Heifetz, R A and Laurie, D L (1997) in 'The work of leadership', *Harvard Business Review*, January-February, Vol. 75 No.1

Kiefer, C (1994) 'Executive team leadership' in Senge, P *et al.*, *The Fifth Discipline Fieldbook*, Nicholas Brealey, London

Kotter, J P (1996) *Leading Change*, Harvard Business School Press, Boston, MA

Laborde, G Z (1987) *Influencing With Integrity*, Syntony Publishing, Palo Alto, CA

Mileham, P and Spacie, K (1996) *Transforming Corporate Leadership*, Pitman Publishing, London

Chapter 5

Developing directors

Learning to fly

IN AT THE DEEP END?

Paul Richmond couldn't wait to get home to tell his wife the good news. He had just been in to see the Managing Director, Tony Johnston who had offered him the job of Production Director of Entirely Electronics. And of course, he had accepted. The position had become available due to the untimely death of Paul's boss and mentor, Brian Jones, who had suffered a heart attack three weeks previously. Entirely Electronics was a medium-sized company which made electronic components. It enjoyed moderate growth and a steady market position because customers could rely on high quality, reliable products at a reasonable cost. The company was also known to be responsive to special customer requests. The company was, however, essentially traditional in character and was beginning to feel the bite of competition, particularly imports from China.

Brian Jones had been the Production Director at Entirely Electronics for nine years and a powerful member of the board as a result of his experience and 35 years with the company, his direct and authoritative manner and his technical expertise. His death left a hole in the board. He had effectively been Tony Johnston's deputy and right-hand man. Brian had been married to his job. He worked long hours, was a hard task master and had an eye for detail. In effect, he had continued to manage production from his position as director via his Production Manager, Paul Richmond.

Paul was 42 and had been with Entirely Electronics for 15 years. He had been recruited by Brian Jones who had acted as his mentor throughout his time with the company. Paul had risen through the production ranks largely because Brian trusted him to do as he was told. He was hard working, experienced and friendly. Production had a good working atmosphere. Everyone had a deep respect for Brian and this helped Paul in his job, as did his affable manner.

Paul's first day as Production Director was a mixture of satisfaction and alarm. He really liked his new office and company car and everyone had been congratulating him on his promotion. He felt that all the years of hard work had paid off – he had finally made it and he was going to enjoy his time as a company director! Apart from a 15-minute chat with Tony Johnston where he had been told that he just needed to continue doing what he was already doing so well and turn up to board meetings, Paul received no training for his new position. There also happened to be a board meeting that day. The other members of the board were Helen Spinks, the Human Resources Director; Matthew Smith, the Finance Director; Zak Seddon, the Sales and Marketing Director; and John Needles, the R&D director. Also at the meeting were the two non-executive directors: Fred Amery, who acted in the capacity of part-time company chairman, and Ronald Bind, a retired businessman.

Paul was welcomed to the board by the chairman and then business began. Paul knew the other board members fairly well, but this was the first time he had witnessed them all working together. He emerged from the meeting feeling profoundly depressed. As he was leaving, Zak Seddon took him to one side to give him some friendly advice. Board meetings, he said, were a necessary evil and the best way to get through them was to keep your head down, your nose clean and offer as little information as possible. Then you could get back to the real job.

Paul went back to his office and made a note of his observations of the meeting.

- Meeting completely dominated by Tony Johnston who made all the decisions and did most of the talking.
- The non-executives were clearly not well informed and a lot of time was wasted with Roland Bind asking for clarification and giving everyone the benefit of his experience.
- The other directors gave a short report about issues in their area which were 'economical'. Matthew Smith gave an honest picture of the company's financial position and tried to raise a number of issues, but was 'blocked' by Tony Johnston.
- Apart from her functional report, Helen Spinks did not utter a word throughout the meeting. Zak Seddon tried to lighten the atmosphere by talking enthusiastically about the impending product launch.
- There was a bitter exchange between Zak Seddon and John Needles about the product launch date, but then they are always fighting.
- Chairman was amiable and managed to get through the agenda to time. But he was not effective at controlling Tony

Johnston (who could not hide his irritation towards Fred) or at making sure the other directors contributed to the meeting.
- Everyone is clearly in awe of Tony and no one challenged him.

Paul, himself, had largely been left alone to observe during the meeting. Nevertheless, he had managed to pick up a large number of actions from Tony: he was going to be very busy until he had appointed a new production manager.

Six months later, Paul Richmond resigned from Entirely Electronics. Becoming a company director had not been anything like he had anticipated. Eager at the beginning, he had done some research into the responsibilities of being a company director. He had been quite unaware of the extent of his legal, financial and fiduciary responsibilities as a director. It had also come as a shock to learn that he was with all the other directors equally responsible for the company's performance. He had tried to contribute as a full board member. In particular, he was concerned that the company was not taking steps to counteract the threat from cheap imports. When he had raised the issue, Tony Johnston had bounced the problem back to him by suggesting that the way out of the problem was for production to lower its costs so that prices could come down. Paul had felt crushed and did not have the confidence to raise the issue again.

He had received little support or help from his colleagues on the board. He had never really felt included or accepted by them and found that he still tended to be deferential towards them, as if he were still only a manager. When he tried to discuss company-wide issues with them, they found it difficult to hide their frustration and lack of interest. As long as everything was going well in their functional areas they were happy. The stress of trying to make a contribution as an equal member of the board in this atmosphere began to show. He became cynical and acted defensively to criticism from whatever source.

Attempting to cope with his discomfort, Paul had thrown himself into operational matters within his function. But this had not turned out as he had expected either. People treated him differently now he was a director. They were not as open or friendly. He found it difficult to establish exactly what was going on without appearing to be interfering unnecessarily. He was aware *that his new production manager was frustrated and tried to keep Paul at arm's length.*

Paul worked long hours but knew he subtracted more value than he added, particularly in his functional area. He did not know what he should be doing differently and the stress was beginning to affect his family life. He did not feel there was anyone he could turn to for advice. He had started to behave like the other directors in board meetings – anything for a quiet life. But this added to his stress because he found it difficult to turn a blind eye to the company's increasingly urgent strategic problems. The board seemed to be content with discussing day-to-day issues especially while the financial results continued their steady improvement.

As a last resort, Paul tried to talk to Tony Johnston. Tony was perplexed by Paul's concerns. He expected Paul to act as Brian had and to be grateful for having been made a director so early in his career. He took Paul's comments as a personal criticism and the meeting ended coolly with Tony suggesting that Paul should concentrate on getting his functional area in order.

The next day, Tony accepted Paul's resignation.

This story is fictional but we do not believe it is untypical. The transition from manager to director is rarely, if ever, smooth. The pleasure of being rewarded with a directorship can soon wear off as the full implications of the role are realized. Few newly appointed directors are prepared for their new role, nor are boards prepared to accept them. When we start a new job we are not instantly effective because we must go up a learning curve. In fact, there are a number of stages within any job which are shown in Figure 11.

Step 1: Induction

The introductory phase of a job, this is concerned mainly with developing a familiarity with the physical surroundings, systems and procedures, and basic factual information required to function in the job. Induction courses for new directors are extremely rare. This reflects the belief that moving from being a senior manager to being a director is nothing more than being a senior manager with a bigger office and more equipment. Research by the Institute of Directors in 1990 showed that 92 per cent of directors

Learning to fly

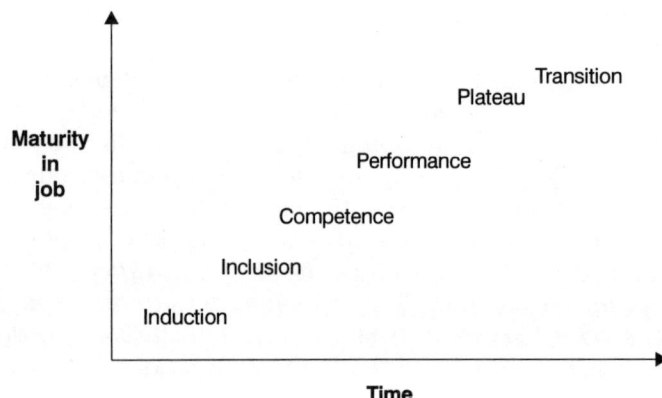

Source: Original by Peter Smith, adapted by Garrett (1996)

Figure 11 Performance stages during the life of a job

had received no training for their directorial role. This is for two main reasons. First, directors believe themselves to have all the necessary skills and knowledge they need otherwise they would not have been made a director. After all, a directorship is a reward for past achievements and current performance. Second, there is a prevailing view that becoming a director does not require any major changes in behaviour or style. There is a belief that you continue to fulfil your functional responsibilities as well as some additional company responsibilities which can be 'picked up' along the way.

Step 2: Inclusion

This is the stage of a job when we are introduced to new colleagues and strive to be accepted by them. In our story, Paul Richmond found he could not progress beyond induction. We cannot move to competence until we have been accepted into the new social grouping. Everyone wants to be included by their social group. Newcomers try to adopt the behaviours of current members in an effort to be accepted. Boards, as a whole, will not be effective until the new member has been included. When new directors are appointed there is often little consideration given to the other

Developing directors

board members. Often highly competitive, other directors can see new members as a threat to their position and consciously or unconsciously resist their inclusion into the group – a classic case of the 'information is power' syndrome. There is also considerable peer and organizational pressure on new directors to conform: to behave in a certain stereotypical way as determined by the culture and behavioural norms of the business and the board. To behave differently requires courage and self-confidence on the part of the new director. This is especially the case when the board is dominated by one individual usually the managing director. New directors often feel isolated. They often know that they are not being as effective as they should, but lack the confidence and know-how to change the situation.

Stage 3: Competence

This comes about when we are confident that we are beginning to make a contribution. Many directors do not move beyond this point because they have adopted the behaviours of the board in order to be accepted. In poorly performing boards this can, in effect, suboptimize directorial performance. Moving to the next stage performance requires confidence and self-belief because it often means having to break out of the confines of the 'behavioural

---

Example 8

Two years ago, a client in the USA was appointed CEO of a business turning over approximately $150 million. This was in an industry where he had a good track record. He was dynamic and creative and was an excellent choice for the position. A year later he was shown the model in Figure 11 and identified with it immediately. He had just resigned his post as CEO because he had not been allowed to make the step to performance. He explained that the previous CEO had been made Chairman but would not let go of the CEO role. So the company had a Chairman acting as a CEO and a CEO acting as a powerful supernumary general manager. As a result of not being able to perform as a CEO, he found he was taking away responsibility and authority from the general managers who were, in turn, taking

Learning to fly

> responsibility away from their direct reports. There was no one fulfilling the role of chairman who might have been able to change the situation. The organization, the chairman, the CEO and the general managers were all suboptimizing their performance. People were not able to express themselves fully within their roles.

box' that other members of the board have dictated.

Stage 4: Performance

It is at this point that we begin to add value. Competence implies sufficiency while performance is the fulfilment of the role. This is the stage that all directors need to aim to reach: the time when creativity and effectiveness are at their highest. If the individual directors and the board, as a whole, are all performing at the same time, excellence and outstanding results can be achieved. It is in order to reach these heights of performance that directors and boards need to be developed.

Stage 5: Plateau

Here people begin to ask themselves, 'Do I stay where I am or do I move on?' They have performed in the role for some time and are no longer as stretched by it as they once were. They are not learning as much or as fast; other people are learning from them. At this stage, people either need to take on a new challenge within the role, develop themselves further in order to bring a new dimension to the role, or leave. People at this point have a great deal to offer newcomers. They make excellent mentors. Another option to consider might be taking on a non-executive director role in another company so that others can benefit from their experience. Frequently, however, the director will move out of the company because the organization has not recognized that he has reached a plateau. This is a good way to lose talent.

Stage 6: Transition

This is the stage of a job when the individual is about to move to another role and knows what that role is. Often they are in the old job in body, but in the new job in spirit. In other words, individuals are unlikely to be highly motivated because they are mentally preparing to move on. However, they have valuable experience and knowledge which should be passed on to others. This is often particularly true of directors. Most companies do not have any form of 'exit policy'. Whether they are leaving the company or being promoted, others can benefit from their experience. This is, of course, particularly true of the successor. One of the consequences of the period of rationalization of business in the UK has been the loss of many middle and senior managers over 50 years old. Companies are beginning to realize now that this has also meant the loss of valuable experience and knowledge that was not passed on.

The higher up the corporate ladder that executives go, the less training and development they receive, despite the increasing complexities of their roles. It is almost as if after the age of 35 or 40 executives know all there is to know. This is, of course, nonsense. Being made a director is seen as the final proof that an executive has what it takes. Besides which, boards are too busy with important matters to take time out to do training. There is also the consideration that the rest of the organization would think it strange that the directors needed training when they are paid to have all the answers. After all, if you are a director you must be the best in the company.

Such attitudes to directorial training reflect a deep misunderstanding of the role of the director. As we discussed in Chapter 3, the difference between being a manager and a director is not a difference in degree; it is a difference in kind. In fact, to become a successful director, an individual needs to stop being a manager. The new director has almost to throw away everything he knew before and begin again. He must acquire the new skills, attitudes and behaviours that will ensure that he, and the other members of the board, provide the organization with the leadership and strategic direction it requires.

Companies need to address the issue of director development as a matter of urgency. A recent survey carried out for Coopers and Lybrand by the University of Warwick Business School and the Foundation for Manufacturing and Industry found that development was not seen as an integral part of company improvement. This was in spite of the fact that a third of respondents felt their

Learning to fly

company's performance was constrained by lack of skills at board level. Only 8 per cent of sample companies provisioned a minimum number of days a year for directors' training. The survey (The Foundation for Manufacturing and Industry, 1997) of 308 medium-sized companies with an annual turnover of between £8m and £500m, concluded that boards suffer a high degree of insularity: they lack breadth and depth as a result of neglecting their own development. At a recent course for company directors we conducted our own straw poll and found that of the 20 participants only two had a budget for personal development, and they were directors of consultancies.

As Figure 12 shows, organizational and people development need to happen in parallel. They are two sides of the same coin. When personal development is high, but there is no ongoing organizational development, people outgrow the business and leave. When organizational development is high, but the investment in developing senior people is low, resistance to change and stress develop, reducing effectiveness. When organizational and personal development is low, so will be morale and the company is more vulnerable to failure. The top right hand box of Figure 12 is the

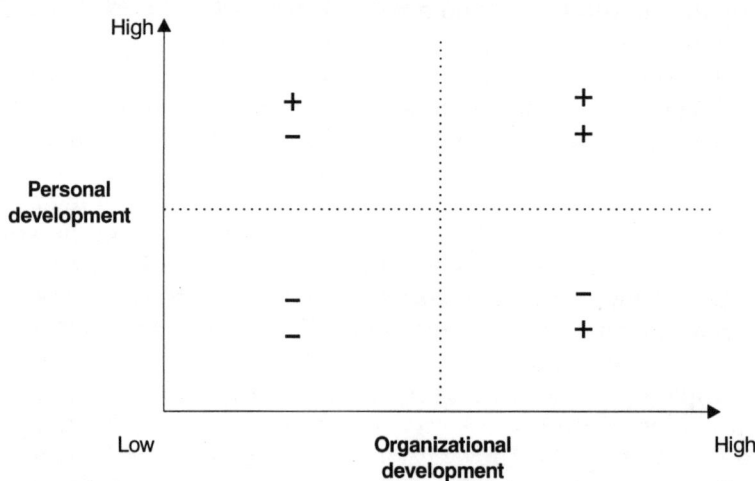

Figure 12 Organizational and personal development work together

only appropriate goal. The development of the organization must be driven by the personal development of its leaders and in the context of its strategy.

Director development and training is not an add-on. It is a prerequisite. Ongoing personal development is an essential element of the directorial role. It is only by continually learning that directors will be able to perform at the level required for organizations to be successful in the future. In addition, the Cadbury Report stated that the training and development of directors is of importance to good corporate governance. The report states that their increasing responsibilities mean that directors should receive some form of training for their role and that new directors should be entitled to some form of induction process. Thus, far from being an opportunity to sit back and enjoy success, becoming a director means making a commitment to life-long learning. It means personal change as a result of acquiring new skills, attitudes and behaviours that allow the individual to direct and lead as opposed to manage.

DEFINING DIRECTOR DEVELOPMENT

The purpose of developing our company directors is to improve their leadership and governance. It involves increasing their skills and knowledge levels, acquiring new and more appropriate behavioural approaches, and enhancing or developing key personal qualities.

The first step is to establish the sorts of knowledge, skills and attributes that directors need to contribute effectively to a performing board. We have described these in some length in Chapters 3 and 4 and they are summarized in Figure 13. The Institute of Directors' *Standards for the Board* also includes a list of qualities that it considers directors need to possess. We should stress that it would be unreasonable to expect every director to be a model of excellence, with all the necessary attributes. What is important is that the board, collectively, aims to have all the required skills and that individual directors are aware of which attributes they have and which they need to develop over time. Figure 13 provides a checklist to which boards and directors can aspire. You will have noticed that functional expertise is not one of the essential directorial skills. Functional expertise is useful when instance, but too much functional focus will actually impede directorial performance.

The list of attributes and knowledge requirements outlined in Figure 13 is not exhaustive nor is it meant to be prescriptive. We offer it merely as a guide or checklist. Boards may like to use it as an initial discussion point with a view to generating their own list of director skills and attributes. They may feel that their industry or the position of their business requires additional directorial qualities.

Knowledge
A full appreciation and understanding of:
- A director's legal, fiduciary, ethical and financial responsibilities
- The workings of the board, including any appropriate codes of best practice
- The purpose of and process for board meetings
- Current thinking on best business practice
- Financial reports and accounting practices
- The company's Memorandum and Articles of Association
- The company's environmental context
- The company's strengths and weaknesses
- The company's vision and strategy
- The perceptions and aspirations of the company's stakeholders

Directorial qualities/attributes
- Strategic thinking
- Commercial focus
- Interpersonal and communication skills
- Ability to be analytical and detail conscious when necessary
- Results oriented
- Team player
- Objectivity

Leadership qualities/attributes
- Communication skills
- Congruence
- Understanding of people
- Confidence
- Personal integrity
- Visionary

Figure 13 Directorial knowledge, skills and attributes

position of their business requires additional directorial qualities.

Alternatively, they may feel that some qualities are more important than others, for their particular business.

Director development encompasses three broad aspects:

- training to gain competence in appropriate areas of knowledge;
- individual development to improve or acquire key personal qualities and behaviours;
- team development of the board to improve performance.

Training

We draw a distinction between training and development. Training aims to improve competence in a particular area. It is essentially task-based and can be standardized because its focus is the job or skill, rather than the person.

> Training is a necessary and often relatively mechanical process by which a blend of knowledge, attitudes and skills is identified to ensure competence in a carefully defined job (Garrett, 1996, pp 190–91).

Directors need training to ensure they achieve competence in the areas of knowledge listed in Figure 13. They should be fully aware of their corporate governance responsibilities, particularly those where they are legally accountable. They should be familiar with how a board functions as well as the specific aspects relating to their company contained in the Memorandum and Articles of Association. Moreover, they should have a working knowledge of the company, its operating environment and general business trends. Such knowledge is not difficult to acquire and should form the basis of an induction programme for any new director.

Since one of the major problems that directors face is lack of diary time, we believe that there is no reason why companies should not design their own simple induction programme for new directors. This has the advantage that it can be tailored to include company-specific information. There could also be supporting information to which directors would then be able to refer. Such an approach will also be useful to help new non-executive directors to familiarize themselves quickly. We have helped clients by conducting director induction programmes or helping them to design their own. The feedback we receive is remarkably consistent. Most newly appointed directors are not aware of the extent of their responsibilities. They often do not realize that in law they share equal responsibility for the company with all the other directors. New directors find induction programmes enormously helpful in the sense that they provide the structural framework for the role. Knowing what is expected of them as directors helps them to begin to make a contribution at board meetings. They are also less likely to make a mistake that could compromise the company's position, or their own.

There may be other areas where training can help directors. Some new directors may be unfamiliar with scrutinizing corporate level financial statements and accounts and might benefit from some form of financial training. One crucial skill or attribute that we have said is an essential requirement for directors is strategic thinking. Many directors we know not only do not think strategically but do not fully understand the concept. This is perhaps because it is often characterized by jargon. There are many excellent training courses offered which can help unravel the jargon and mystery of strategy. This is an area, for instance, where business schools often excel. Since the ability to think strategically is one of the hallmarks of being a director, this is an area of training that should not be neglected.

What little is on offer to help improve directors' performance is mostly in the area of training. In an effort to lure this notoriously reluctant group of people, business schools and other training establishments have started to tailor their courses so that they are more company-specific and practical. Many directors have a natural antipathy towards esoteric or general courses. They have little time to spare and find off-site general training of little long-term value. It is only relatively recently that a training distinction has begun to be drawn between the needs of managers and the needs of directors. More often courses are being offered which combine theoretical input with participant interaction. Many directors, particularly chief executives, find this useful because they often feel isolated and this provides an opportunity to interact with and learn from peers. As the *Financial Times* (20 March 1997) described:

> ...the course is likely to have a 'facilitator' who brings the executives together and helps steer discussions. Meetings of this kind trade on the theme that it is 'lonely at the top' and that chief executives have no one to talk their ideas through with.

Some directors value the opportunity to get away from the business for a short time. It helps them to gain some perspective on their company. They also value the opportunity to meet and learn from other people. However, the majority of directors resist going on training courses citing lack of time as the principal reason. The real reason is often that directors do not find off-site standard training courses sufficiently relevant. In this sense, they may not always be good value for money since what is learned may not be applied and is quickly forgotten when the director returns to the office. One way to combat this is for companies to organize in-house, tailored courses for all their directors. These will tend to be related to the company and new skills are more likely to be practised when everyone has been trained. We have found that clients are increasingly asking us to organize and run these sorts of tailored directors' courses.

Development

Development focuses on the person, rather than the job. It is concerned with realizing potential. Personal development is about the individual gaining a better understanding of themselves, the way they behave in certain situations, and the way they conduct their relationships. This self-knowledge provides the basis from which to learn new approaches and develop new attitudes which will provide them with the behavioural flexibility to respond more effectively to different situations. It is through the process of personal development that directors will acquire, or become more proficient in, the key directorial and leadership skills listed above in Figure 13. Directors need to accept the necessity of ongoing personal development to help them grow into the directorial role. This is the process that will help them to develop the variety of thinking styles and behavioural approaches needed to tackle the diversity of issues with which boards are confronted.

Training is often a passive process of receiving and absorbing information. Personal development is quite different. The individual can only benefit if he has made a commitment to learning and improving. He must take ownership for his own development as nobody else can do it for him. Once an individual has made a commitment to personal development, significant change is possible with suitable support and encouragement. Humanistic psychologists would argue that personal growth and the search for self-actualization or self-fulfilment is a fundamental human drive. Whether or not you agree with this, it is certainly the case that people always have greater potential within them than they are currently realizing. Their performance and, therefore, the company's performance can be improved dramatically.

There are a number of personal development methods or approaches available. Directors may decide to undertake their own development. Some people have an in-built need to keep learning and will take every opportunity to expose themselves to new experiences. They will read books, put themselves through external development courses, and may even see a personal counsellor. There are many personal development courses available. Most are focused on helping individuals to realize their own potential in the spiritual sense but a few offer the perspective of the business context. Most personal development approaches work from the premise that the individual has the resources he needs to make changes within himself but that he may need help to access these resources. One danger that can arise when an individual embarks on a personal development programme is that he finds he needs to face issues in his past. Incidents in our past will have shaped our behaviours today. When we are trying to change behaviour we can discover that the reason for our current behaviour is no longer appropriate or is painful to face. Thus, when embarking on a personal development programme, the director needs to be aware that he may have to confront difficult personal issues in order to move forward.

Personal development means personal change. Very often people find that they go through a transformation. They need to be aware that while they may have changed, other people around them will not have. Their family and work colleagues will find the changes in a person they thought they knew well confusing and disorientating. It is important, therefore, when going through personal change to consider the effect upon your relationships, both business and personal.

Self-managed learning is one approach to personal development. The drawback from an organizational point of view is that this development does not take place within the context of the business. There are methods for developing directors within the organizational context. Some companies use structured assessment centres to benchmark current performance with the output being a personal development plan which may involve a combination of external courses and internal job rotation, for instance. Short-term job rotations or exchanges can be another method of developing a wider perspective and depth of experience.

Mentoring is used in a number of organizations. This is where a senior, more experienced person is assigned to be a mentor to one or more other people. His role is to provide advice and guidance on company-related, but not usually job-related, issues. The most usual advice given is about career direction. Part of the role of the mentor is to act as a role model.

By far the most effective form of director development is coaching. Coaching is different from mentoring in that it is more interactive. The coach facilitates the individual to solve his own problems and orchestrate his own learning. There are a number of different coaching approaches. Much of our work with clients is concerned with coaching individual senior managers and directors. Chapter 6 gives a description of our coaching approach supported by client experiences.

Team Development

The development of directors and the board needs to be a planned and conscious process. To be most effective, the development of individual directors must happen within the context of the development of the board as a whole and within the context of the business. Developing directors in a vacuum will only exacerbate the problems of a non-performing board as it will accentuate the existing divisions. While the individual director may well benefit from personal development, the overall performance of the board will only improve if all the directors are being developed within an agreed framework.

Thus, the starting point for director development is an honest and open assessment of the board's individual and collective strengths and weaknesses within the context of the requirements of the business at the time. The outcome of such an assessment will provide the benchmark against which future performance improvements can be measured. Boards will usually require external help when undertaking this process. This is the basis from which a board development plan will emerge which must apply to all directors, including the non-executives, the chief executive and the chairman.

In addition to developing its collective skills and attributes, the board needs to develop as a team. A team can be defined as a group of people coming together for a common purpose. This sounds straightforward but often people within a team begin with a different perspective of what their common purpose is. A starting point for any team development of the board of directors, then, is for all to agree what the common purpose is.

Why should boards become teams? Anyone who has been a member of a truly performing team, whether on the sports field or at work, will know the levels of energy, creativity and commitment that are achievable. This is what boards need to help them to inspired performance. This is the level that must be reached if ongoing corporate renewal is to be achieved. Unfortunately, teams rarely happen just by putting a group of people together in the same room. What is more likely to occur is a co-operative group. Co-operative groups can perform well but, because they accommodate conflict and focus only on the task without considering group processes, outstanding performance is unlikely. The lack of trust and openness leads to group dynamics, such as politics, which waste time and energy. If you are in a rowing team and the two members of your team at the back collude to row differently from everyone else, the boat will not get very far.

In effective teams trust is high, feelings are expressed freely and commitment is high. The dynamics of how the team works together are considered important and part of the work. Differences between members are valued to the extent that each member has a team role which others accept. For instance, some people are good at generating ideas while others are able to detect the potential flaws in a plan. In a co-operative group, these two team types would frustrate each other. In a performing team each can see the contribution the other makes to the whole. People are open in effective teams. Thus, conflict is brought out into the open and worked through. Ultimately, conflict will be seen as a useful dynamic which, turned positively, can help the overall creativity of the team.

To develop an effective team takes time, courage, persistence and effort. The group of individuals have to go through a number

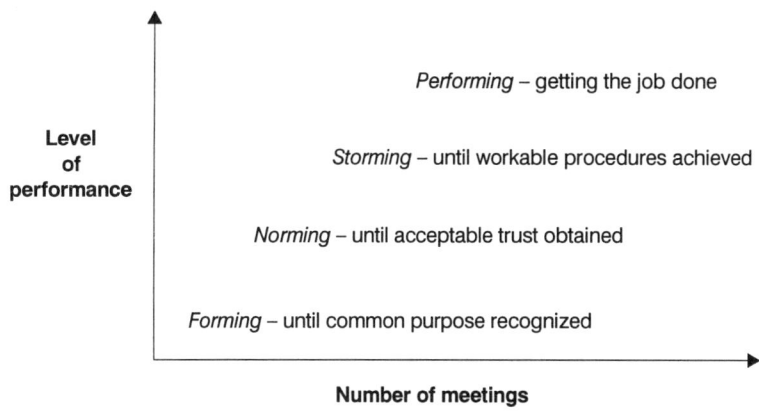

Figure 14 Team development stages

of learning stages before they will be able to perform. Figure 14 shows the main stages of team development.

Team development cannot take place unless, at the outset, all the directors have agreed that they want to participate in a board and personal development process. This is because it requires a commitment to being open and to developing a level of trust that will make the board a more effective working group. For many directors this can be an uncomfortable process. They need to share aspects of themselves they would normally keep private and admit to weaknesses. Most directors are used to concealing their weaknesses and to being confrontational rather than collaborative. Initially, in any form of team or individual development process, some directors can become extremely frustrated. They are pushed into doing things that make them deeply uncomfortable and often have difficulty relating the process to the needs of the business. They just want to 'get on with the job'. They tend to be task focused and find it difficult to see the connection between nebulous concepts such as building trust and moving the organization forward. The board should, therefore, be clear about why it needs to develop and what it is aiming to develop towards.

There are a number of alternative ways of building effective teams, ranging from outdoor 'survival' courses to facilitated open discussions aimed at building trust and improving relationships.

Learning to fly

The purpose of outdoor courses is to take people out of their working environment where they tend to be trapped into predictable behaviour patterns. People are then put into situations of discomfort and difficulty in order to force them to work together for the common good. Such courses can be highly successful but have some drawbacks. First, because they are so out of the work context the initial euphoria felt can dissipate over time. Second, they work best where groups are relatively evenly balanced in terms of age and fitness. Third, people in a group who are active and maybe fitter than the rest of the group are unlikely to benefit as much as others because they are less likely to find themselves in a position where they have to trust a colleague to help them. Fourth, they tend to bring out competitive rather than collaborative behaviours. Finally, the environment is sometimes seen as being too different from the workplace for the lessons learned to be sufficiently relevant.

Another way to build teams is by using a skilled internal or external person to facilitate the team development stages. Psychometric tests can be a useful tool in such approaches as a way of helping to build understanding and trust. Individual scores are taken but the emphasis is on the pattern for the team as a whole.

This can be an extremely enlightening process for directors and can immediately and dramatically improve relationships. The 'scientific' nature of psychometric tests provides a way of depersonalizing and legitimizing a debate about people's personalities and working styles. They are useful for prompting a debate about the differences between people. While we would not advise an over-reliance on psychometric tests, we do believe them to be a useful method of prompting a debate about the differences and similarities between people in a neutral way. It is not about one person's opinion of another; it is about comparing people against a consistent and objective set of criteria. There are a number of excellent tests that can be used which are easy to use and score. The important thing is to use tests which are appropriate such as those which look at preferred styles of working.

Using psychometric tests can also help to benchmark objectively a board's current spread of skills and abilities. They can be used to initiate a discussion among directors about the differences between them and how the board might benefit from these differences. A third benefit is that they often help directors to understand the dynamics of their relationships with their colleagues. This helps to reduce tension and animosity. Differences become valued and respected. Finally, directors start to learn from each other. Gaining a better understanding of yourself and your fellow directors is the key to building trust and improved relationships. When two individuals clash, it is usually a huge relief for both to discover that they are opposite personality types. It provides a reason for the conflict and a neutral basis for the two to discuss their differences without seeming to criticise personally. People intellectually know that everyone is different. In reality, however, they behave as if they assume everyone thinks as they do. An appreciation of different types of people and different working styles leads to greater tolerance and a respect for others' points of view without feeling personally threatened.

To rely solely on psychometric tests alone would be dangerous. They are a useful tool within the context of a structured discussion led by skilled and objective facilitators. We frequently use them in our work with clients. By themselves, they can be less useful. There can be an inclination to box and label people as 'such-and-such' a personality type, thereby oversimplifying and trivializing complex personality differences. In addition, certain organizational cultures will value some personality types more highly than others. The danger is that people will be seen as having the 'right' personality or the 'wrong' personality. This can be divisive since personality is relatively fixed. The important thing is that having a certain personality will lead people to behave in different ways. A skilled facilitator will ensure that the discussion is aimed at an understanding and appreciation of the differences between individuals and does not degenerate into a debate about whether one personality type is 'better' than another.

The method that we use in our work to build boards into effective teams is based on coaching techniques. The emphasis is on collectively agreeing the board's purpose, assessing its collective ability to achieve that purpose and coaching individuals and the group to make the necessary changes to ensure it happens. Using coaching is a way of achieving individual and board development in parallel within the strategic framework of the business. Thus, development is relevant and focused. We discuss our approach to coaching boards in greater detail in Chapter 7.

> **Example 9**
>
> In one client organization the interplay between one-to-one coaching and group coaching was very effective. The organization was going through a change programme and we were brought in to help build the team responsible for driving the change. Trust, openness and co-operation were low. As coaches we acted initially as conduits for communication between people when they did not feel able to communicate directly. People used to tell us privately what they thought of their colleagues until they could find the right words and the courage to talk directly to each other. Over time they began to be able to deal with conflict and confront difficult issues by themselves which allowed them to work together through change. The one-to-one coaching sessions provided a safe environment for the individuals to work out how to build their relationships with each other.

WHO IS RESPONSIBLE FOR DEVELOPING DIRECTORS?

The chairman is responsible for the performance of the board and, therefore, is also the person responsible for its development. By implication, the chairman should also ensure that all the directors are trained and developed. The chief executive or managing director, by contrast, is responsible for the strategic performance of the business. Thus, while it is the chairman's role with the non-executive directors to advise, coach and develop other members of the board, the chief executive and his team execute strategy. To take a footballing analogy, the chairman is the team manager while the chief executive is the captain on the field and the other directors are the players. This analogy helps to explain why it is essential that the role of chairman and chief executive or managing director are separated. It is virtually impossible to be the team manager, captain and a player. The same is true in business.

As the head of the board, the chairman has the corporate governance role for ensuring that the board and its members are developed. However, the responsibility for the personal development of directors really belongs with the directors themselves.

To achieve ongoing growth and development, directors must make a personal commitment. In other words, directors should not use a chairman who is not organizing personal development for directors as an excuse for not undertaking any. Ideally, individual director development is a partnership between the chairman and the directors. The chairman provides the resources and encouragement as well as ensuring that all training and development activities are relevant within the context of the board's overall development and the company's strategic direction. The director is responsible for benchmarking his skills, competences and attributes; for identifying his weak areas and for ensuring he receives appropriate support to help him improve in these. One of the chairman's tasks is then to monitor the developmental progress of each director.

Recruitment and Selection

This is an area where the chairman must take a lead but the whole board should be involved. There is a tendency to recruit new directors in a vacuum. They are selected for their functional specialism and their experience, as opposed to their directorial ability or fit with the board team.

Example 10

We were involved recently with a client organization that had little experience with director recruitment and selection. Following a restructuring they recruited a new director to head a newly created division. The choice turned out to be a disastrous mistake. The new director's style was abrasive. He upset people inside the company as well as clients to the point where they all refused to work with him. He was so competitive that he exposed his colleagues in board meetings in order to receive glory himself. At this time, all the other members of the board were participating in a coaching programme but this individual refused to take part. After six months the new director's contract was terminated.

The example above, we feel, proves the point that when selecting new directors major consideration should be taken of the fit with the rest of the team. This is not to say that new directors should be recruited on the basis that they are the same or like the other directors. Far from it. The aim is for the board to have a clear picture of its collective strengths and weaknesses and to bring in new people who can complement the existing blend of skills. Ideally, the new individual will be different from everyone else and have strengths in areas where the board is collectively weak. Functional expertise is of lesser importance. At the same time, it is important that the new director complements the team in terms of personal values and style of working. It is no good being so different that the effects are like the example above.

The recruitment and selection of new directors is a critically important aspect of director development to get right. It is something that chairmen and boards should take time over. The arrival of a new 'different' director who is willing and able to challenge the board's thinking will be of immense value. The chairman is responsible for the recruitment process but the whole board must participate in the decision. This helps to test out the fit of a new person within the existing team and to gain acceptance, part of the inclusion process we discussed earlier. Other points to remember when recruiting a new director are:

- Recruit for what the business will need in the future, not just what it needs today – do you need a visionary or an administrator?
- When recruiting to replace a departing director, challenge whether you actually need a like-for-like replacement – is this an opportunity to create a new, more appropriate role on the board or is it needed at all?
- If you are recruiting internally, make sure it is not just a reward for long service but that it is based on merit – will the person add value and what will be the consequences of removing him from his current role?
- Pursue references for external candidates and do not rely on interviews alone – do you need professional outside help?
- Make sure you have an induction process – what do you need to do to ensure the new director is able to perform as early as possible?
- Make sure that you are not recruiting someone in your own image.

When we talk about the importance of recruiting people who bring something different to the board, we are not confining this difference to a way of thinking or a particular attribute. The chairman must ensure that the board is not tempted (for all sorts of good reasons) to shy away from recruiting someone who will really provide a challenge and stimulus. A different perspective can come from a number of directions. For instance, the board of a new, dynamic high-tech company populated by young directors might benefit from recruiting an older director who can bring experience and stability. Equally, a board populated by men only might benefit from recruiting a woman. To break through the 'glass ceiling' many women have had to dampen down some of their more natural tendencies and adopt the behaviours of their male colleagues. This is fortunately changing, albeit slowly. While it is an arguable point, women can bring another perspective and a different dimension, as a result of different life experiences, and it would appear that boards are beginning to realize this. A recent survey by the Institute of Management found that the number of women at board level increased from 3.3 per cent in 1996 to 4.5 per cent in 1997. In addition, women directors' pay rose by 9.2 per cent on average compared with 7.8 per cent for male directors (Institute of Management, 1997).

Induction and Training for Non-Executive Directors

In terms of board development the chairman should ensure that non-executive directors make a full contribution. This means that consideration is given to their training and development. Perhaps the most critical stage for a non-executive director is his introduction to the company. This means that for them to be effective, they too require an induction process. Indeed, because they only serve part-time, their induction could be more extensive than for new executive directors who are able to find things out later. For instance, non-executive directors might visit key company sites, have an opportunity to meet and speak with staff, meet key customers and suppliers, as well as spending time 'shadowing' executive directors. Their induction package could include board minutes for at least six months, the strategic and business plans, an appointment contract, and a copy of any relevant reports relating to board activities. Finally boards should consider assigning a more experienced non-executive director to act as mentor for the time it takes the new non-executive to settle into his role.

Non-executive directors' skills and attributes must be assessed. Training and development should be arranged so that non-executive directors are an equal members of the board and can function effectively as an independent voice. As with executive directors, non-executive directors should have a personal development plan which forms a basis for review. Companies rarely consider non-executive directors when thinking about directors' development.

> What so often happens, when a senior figure is approached to join the board as an independent director, is that both sides are too embarrassed to raise the subject of competence and training. What is essentially a failure of courage and frankness on both sides can give rise to major problems later (Clutterbuck and Waine, 1994, p 92).

Appraisal and Review

In a team of equals, the management of the review of performance is difficult. It is neglected by many companies with the result that effectively the board is not accountable. This is a corporate governance issue. Boards need to monitor their individual and collective performance to show themselves and others that they are carrying out their directorial duties. Most directors have objectives to meet and these may be incentivized with bonuses. However, these objectives are often ill-defined and general, relating to overall company performance rather than the individual's peformance or that of the board. Boards need to be seen to be accountable for their performance. Targets need to be set which measure the performance of the board itself, not just the company. Aspects of the board's work that could be measured might include, for instance, team development progress, improved board communications, resolution of critical strategic issues, and number of director training days. The aim of developing directors is to improve their effectiveness and that of the board. There is little point in a board embarking on a sophisticated director development programme unless a benchmark is taken at the beginning and progress is reviewed along the way. The chairman must regularly ask the question, 'Are we improving our individual and collective effectiveness at decision making, investment choices, risk analysis, learning and so on? And what is the evidence to support this?'

Further, the chairman should disseminate this evidence not only to employees, but also to customers and shareholders.

The organization's strategy will determine the corporate objectives. These objectives cascade down the organization to ensure that the strategy is implemented. Good strategic management requires that people's personal objectives are closely linked to the company strategy. In addition, the chairman should set performance targets for the board itself which will cascade to individual directors. Ideally, while the chairman is responsible for the process, the board should collectively agree its performance criteria. Directors' performance measures should include 'hard' targets, such as strategy-related objectives, shareholder value, competitiveness and so on, and 'soft' targets, such as progress on their personal development plan. Some directors we have worked with, for instance, have aimed to improve the way they communicate, relate to clients and delegate.

Again the process for assessing how individual directors are performing against their targets should be the responsibility of the chairman. However, directors should take responsibility for assessing their own performance. One very effective way of receiving feedback is using a 360° appraisal. As the name implies, this is a managed process for getting constructive feedback from all levels of staff: direct reports, bosses, peers, customers and suppliers where appropriate. It is an open process which might be one of the only sources of feedback for a director on how he is doing. It is useful for finding out what you are doing well as much as for areas that you need to improve.

> ### Example 11
> During one coaching assignment we worked with an individual who had board potential by virtue of his seniority and length of service with the company. However, his style was a problem. He was not a team player. He was a poor delegator, tending to 'dump the dross'. He viewed information as power so his staff felt that they were 'being treated like mushrooms' and kept in the dark. One of us coached him on a one-to-one basis for six months. Together we set very specific objectives for the things that needed to be changed and monitored progress by getting 360° feedback. The individual is now a main board director and a different person.

Learning to fly

External Help

In the area of director development, a major task for the chairman will be managing specialist, external expertise. Much of the task is achievable using internal people and some boards may feel that they can develop themselves by themselves. However, external expertise brings a number of benefits:

- an objective perspective;
- experience from other organizations;
- skills, ideas, techniques and models;
- a reason to do it (because you are paying and have committed time);
- a sounding-board for participants.

The reality, then, is that external consultants can be useful for developing boards, especially in the early days. However, the chairman must manage this expertise so that the benefits are long term. A consultancy approach that is too prescriptive will only have short-term benefits because the board will not 'own' the solution. Likewise, relying solely on internal expertise, such as internal facilitators or coaches to help people produce their own solutions, does not bring new ideas or challenge existing thinking. Our approach is illustrated in Figure 15. Our belief is that greatest long-term value is achieved by balancing internal and external expertise. We use coaching to pull solutions from individuals combined with consultancy to push new ideas and concepts to help move the team forward. We have found that this method achieves the quantum leaps in development that boards need.

Succession Planning

Another aspect of director development that chairmen need to concern themselves with is where are the directors of the future? We have seen many organizations where there is a strong, highly respected director only a few years from retirement and no one with their calibre to replace them. Boards are often aware that they have a problem but decide not to tackle it until they are forced to; probably in the hope that the problem will go away!

Developing directors

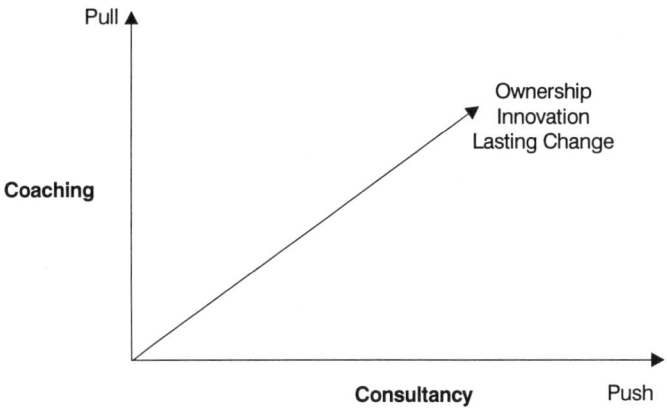

Figure 15 Balancing internal and external expertise

Meanwhile, there are usually senior managers in organizations who aspire to becoming a director. In the absence of any formal way of showing their aspirations, these managers may resort to organizational politics and other covert tactics to help them achieve their goal. Figure 16 was given to us by one of our clients. It offers more constructive suggestions.

- Take responsibility   } take accountability and be given
- Assume authority   } the chance to prove themselves
- Expand their own boundaries by pushing out at the soft spots to see where it takes them
- Receive training on the legislative requirements of directorship
- Have a senior manager forum (one level down from the board)
- Practice at directing
- Interact with directors and be treated on level terms
- See themselves as extensions to directors' arms rather than artificial limbs
- Maintain the grass roots contacts and other sources of information
- Be innovative and not confrontational

Figure 16 What senior managers aspiring to become directors want

Learning to fly

Formal succession planning is rare in companies but essential, especially for directors. Where boards are performing well, it is important that continuity be maintained. Identifying and developing potential future directors helps to minimize disruption for the board ensuring that it maintains its effectiveness. It also ensures that new directors are fully cognizant of the responsibilities they face as directors before assuming the position. This means they can be fully effective more quickly. Developing future directors also means that companies are more likely to select new directors from within the organization, than have to look outside.

Total Wellbeing

Organizational life is highly stressful, especially at director level. Companies often have very closed cultures so that there is a marked separation between home life and organizational life. Showing feelings, talking about one's family and looking after oneself are not familiar concepts in many companies. The 'macho' style of management lives on. All directors, prompted by the chairman, owe it to themselves and their shareholders to take care of themselves. Directors have enormous responsibilities which are becoming increasingly arduous. Learning and developing is more likely to happen if the individual gives himself permission to make the time and space. This means having physical and mental energy. We believe that directors need to take an holistic approach to their development. One aspect they might consider, for instance, is their level of physical fitness.

Example 12

Our client was a senior manager in a peripheral part of a company. Due to technological and market changes this small 'backwater' became the most important single department within the business. Before the change, the department never originated or delivered more than one strategically important project each year. Now it became the place where the majority of strategic initiatives originated and were implemented with great success. At the end of the year our client received an excellent appraisal, enlarged responsibility and was

> more confident and less stressed than he was at the beginning. He was asked what some of the important events during the coaching process were. One of the answers was surprising from someone who had accomplished so much. He said an important item was an almost 'throw-away' comment made by his coach regarding fitness and stamina. He had bought himself a mountain bike for two reasons: to increase his general fitness and to spend some time on Saturday mornings with his sons. 'It was,' he said 'the start of a fitness programme which eventually gave me an extra hour of peak performance a day so that I could stay on top of all the changes going on and feel that I was staying in control of the situation.' The extra hour, five days a week was essential.

When coaching, we encourage individuals to take a more rounded view of their lives. After all, we only get one chance at this thing called 'life' and we should try to enjoy as much of it as we can!

PERSONAL DEVELOPMENT ACTION PLAN

As we said earlier, personal development of directors is an essential element of the directorial role. New directors, in effect, make a commitment to life-long learning. While many directors may accept this principle, they may find it harder to know where to start. We offer some suggestions below of actions that can be taken immediately.

1. Assess yourself as objectively as possible against the knowledge and attributes criteria in Figure 13. You may like to ask the opinion of colleagues, family and direct reports. Use the information to give yourself a personal benchmark and to compile a list of development needs.
2. On the basis of these development needs prepare a personal development plan. Set yourself development targets or objectives. Discuss the plan with your chairman (or whoever is responsible for director development within your organization) to get his support, suggestions and, if necessary, funding.

If there is no one taking a lead for development in your organization, pursue your plan independently.
3. Discuss with your board colleagues the idea of putting together an induction programme for new directors (including non-executive directors).
4. Set aside a minimum number of days per month in your diary for 'personal development'. These may be used for courses, reading, reflection or receiving coaching, for instance.
5. Initiate a 360° appraisal process. As a minimum this should be for yourself, but you should also try to persuade other directors to join you.
6. Initiate a board discussion on how best the board might develop itself with a view to improving its performance.
7. Try to assess your contribution to the board. What team role do you tend to adopt? Think of another director to whom you find it difficult to relate. What team role does he contribute to the board? What value does this have and can you learn from it?
8. Arrange a social evening for all board members, including non-executives, to help break down barriers and develop relationships.
9. Assess your level of personal fitness. Should you be taking more exercise? Think what you would like to do if you had the time, and do it anyway.
10. Initiate personal development plans for your direct reports. Are any of them potential future directors? Could they be with sufficient help and development?

References

Clutterbuck, D and Waine, P (1994) *The Independent Board Director: Selecting and Using the Best Non-Executive Directors to Benefit Your Business*, McGraw-Hill Book Company, London

Financial Times (1997) 20 March

Garrett, B (1996), *The Fish Rots From the Head*, HarperCollins Business, London

Institute of Management (1997) *Remuneration Economics*, reported in the *Financial Times*, 16 June

The Foundation for Manufacturing and Industry (1997) *The Middle Market; How They Perform; Education, Training and Development*, as quoted in the *Financial Times*, 4 June

Chapter 6

The case for coaching

'GIANTS WHO BELIEVE THEY ARE DWARFS'

Coaching is a method of personal development that works from the premise that a person's potential is virtually unlimited. What constrains our performance is self-doubt and our limiting perception of our capabilities – 'giants who believe they are dwarfs' (as quoted by one of our clients Rob Alderman). The coaching process works by challenging these self-limiting beliefs about what we can and cannot do. In this way we open ourselves to the possibility of learning to do new things and tackle difficulties that previously we would have avoided. The aim is to help the individual being coached to find the resources within himself to make the changes necessary in order to realize his long-term goals.

In the last chapter we stressed the importance of director development for the future success of organizations. Directors need to accept the necessity of ongoing personal development to help them grow into the directorial role. We discussed a variety of training and development methods that are available to enable directors to acquire the skills and capabilities they need to tackle today's business issues. Of these, by far the most effective form of director development is coaching. Technical and professional training improves performance by five to ten per cent if you are lucky: coaching, if done well, can improve performance by literally hundreds of per cent.

Coaching aims to achieve relevant, focused organizational learning and growth by concentrating on the personal development of its organizational leaders. In our experience, it is the most effective method for closing the gap between the rate of change occurring in the business environment and the speed of change in organizational and executive development. One reason for this is that coaching is essentially practical. People learn by tackling business issues as they arise.

We do not claim that coaching is a panacea. As a method of personal development it is complete and can stand alone. It is often the only form of development our clients experience. It can also sit alongside other complementary forms of director development and can help to place these in context. For instance, one of our coaching clients recently began the Institute of Directors' Diploma course in company direction. During the coaching session, she was asked how she would share her learning with her board colleagues; something that she had not thought about previously. When coaching sits alongside other forms of training it realizes even greater benefits from that training as the whole emphasis of coaching is on realizing you are learning and helping to identify ways in which that learning can be applied practically.

We have coached individuals and groups in organizations for the last ten years. During that time we have seen some remarkable transformations both of individuals and organizations, as a direct result. Moreover, it is a long-term approach because people generally continue self-coaching after the programme has finished. In some cases, clients have internalized the coaching approach as part of their management style and repertoire of influencing skills. This approach encourages learning and is useful for directors learning to become new leaders.

In order to legitimize and evidence our beliefs about coaching as an effective form of personal development for directors, we have used direct quotes from some of our coaching clients, most of whom are directors.

WHAT IS COACHING?

Coaching revolves around a one-to-one confidential relationship between a skilled coach and a client that lasts for about a year.

> Coaching aims to enhance the performance and learning ability of others. It involves providing feedback, but it also uses other techniques such as motivation, effective questioning and consciously matching your management style to the coachee's readiness to undertake a particular task. It is based on helping the coachee to help him/herself through dynamic interaction – it does not rely on a one-way flow of telling and instructing (Landsberg, 1996, p xi).

The client (the individual being coached) takes full responsibility for his own personal development. Coaching is not something that is done to him. The relationship between coach and client is a partnership. The client owns the issues or the content and the coach owns the process. The coach has ultimate responsibility for the efficacy of the partnership. He ensures that there is a structure, that the coaching sessions do not ramble off the point and that the client's objectives for the process are achieved.

Learning to fly

While in a coaching session, the coach's total attention and focus is on the individual client. However, his ultimate responsibility is to the organization. Coaching sessions always take place within the framework of the organization's aspirations. The prerequisite to any coaching programme, then, is an assessment of the company's strategic objectives. What are the implications of the strategy for the behaviours and actions of the organization's employees, particularly the directors? Usually this means organizational and personal change. The model of change that we use frequently, we have referred to earlier on p. 62. The four stages of change are:

1. *Denial* – When confronted with change our first response as human beings is to deny the necessity for it. Coaching people in denial is about gently and persistently confronting them with the new reality; the way things are now.
2. *Resistance* – The next phase of the process is when we have to come to terms with the actuality of change but we do not like it, so our response is to resist. At this stage the best approach is to do more listening than talking so that people have the opportunity to come to their own conclusions that things are indeed changing whether they like it or not.
3. *Exploration* – At this stage we are willing to explore new ways of doing things in the new regime, new culture or new situation in which we find ourselves. In terms of coaching, it is often best to keep a narrow focus with lots of small steps as some people are inclined to explore too widely and try too many different options before coming through to their version of commitment. Others may feel that a wider perspective should be taken in the exploration phase, but we have found that in their enthusiasm people have a tendency to start too many projects which they fail to complete. This may eventually result in a drop in self-esteem, a feeling that 'this isn't working' and a return to resistance.
4. *Commitment* – This is a full acceptance and embracing of the new circumstances. At this point people can help others to move through the change cycle.

People's reaction to change is not entirely predictable. People can move from denial to resistance and back again. However, handled professionally, people can be encouraged to move through the

The case for coaching

change cycle more quickly and with less trauma than might otherwise occur. Some people may never reach commitment. The coach's job when working with a board is to make sure that everyone who can reaches commitment as quickly as possible. This is because the change process will move at the speed of the slowest *crucial* person. We have found using this diagnostic model combined with the coaching approach to be a highly effective way of facilitating organizational change. The coach acts as a catalyst. As we have said earlier, ongoing organizational change or renewal is the goal. True organizational change will only happen when it becomes embedded in the culture which requires the organization's people to have changed their behaviour and attitudes.

Personal change can be extremely traumatic for some people who find living with ambiguity uncomfortable. For others a life of continuous change is exciting and stimulating. For all of us, however, change brings a degree of stress which can be relieved by knowing that it is a natural process, by understanding what is happening to us and by having someone help us to deal with it and learn from it.

An important point to stress is that coaching is not remedial. Coaching should not be confused with therapy or counselling. The focus is firmly on the positive and the future. The focus of counselling, meanwhile, is generally on the past: dealing with today's problems by going back in the client's past and exorcizing the cause in order to free the client to behave differently today. Part of the coach's responsibility is to ensure that the focus of the sessions is on the future.

Coaching considers the whole person. In business today there is a tendency, especially at senior levels, for people to compartmentalize their lives. Our experience of most organizational cultures is that, once at work, an individual's family life is not recognized or 'allowed in' except in times of emergency. Feelings tend to be switched off or ignored. Behaviours which would not be acceptable in a social situation are seen as the norm in a business context. This has the effect of sustaining the 'macho' style of organizational behaviour which is not conducive to learning. Such compartmentalization is not sustainable in the long term. Nor is it a fulfilling way of working. Corporate renewal is about learning and creativity. These will only flourish where people are allowed to express themselves. People will learn and perform most effectively when their life is in balance or in harmony. A disproportionate

Learning to fly

attention to work can lead to intolerance and a narrow band of behavioural responses to situations. Many directors we know work very long hours at the expense of their families and, sometimes, their health. They feel it is expected of them; that they need to be in control. However, time spent does not necessarily equate with effectiveness nor does the desire to be in control show trust in managers' capabilities. In fact, the long-term consequences of being a 'workaholic' are usually that business issues are out of proportion and out of context. Directors struggle to keep a healthy strategic view. As one managing director put it:

> ...you have much more confidence in dealing with not just work issues but home issues as well...I've managed to stand back a bit from business and that's been good. You can be a workaholic and it just doesn't do you or your family or the business any good.

Coaching takes an holistic approach. The coach helps the individual to balance the various roles that we all have to play in our lives: leader, work colleague, mother or father, friend, daughter or son and so on. The coach will help the individual assess the impact of one part of his life on another. There may be situations or events in a person's personal life that hold clues as to how they might tackle a difficult business issue, for instance. The coach will also help the individual to explore their feelings and how these might drive their actions. One of our coaching clients described it as:

> ... a useful process to go through to actually examine how do I feel in certain situations and how does it impact on the way I approach things and the way I work?

Some might say that coaching is 'selfish' in the sense that the whole focus of attention is on the client as an individual. We would argue that it is 'selfing'. The aim of coaching is self-actualization: to find out what you really want as an individual rather than what you think you ought to want. The model in Figure 17 is a useful way of explaining this. The aim is to get through the outer rings to the inner ring. A person will demonstrate where they are in the model by the sort of language they use. For example, a person in the outer ring will use phrases like, 'I should...' or 'I ought...' Moving to the next stage is difficult because people must confront the fear that they may really be someone they do not want to be. However, this

The case for coaching

is a necessary stage to discovering just what it is that you do want from life. A managing director said:

> ... he does challenge you to come up with your own self-assessment to use as a base to move on from, and the first thing you find normally is that it is not what it really is but what you would like it to be or how you would like others to think of you. So I think the most challenging part was finding out and saying, 'well, I'm this kind of person', which provided the base from which to move on.

At this point the person is clear about his goals and comfortable with pursuing them. He stops wasting energy on activities that he can now see as peripheral.

Usually such a process happens within the context of the organization. However, sometimes, the individual will decide that what they really want lies outside their current organization. It is usually beneficial for the individual and the organization to find this out sooner rather than later.

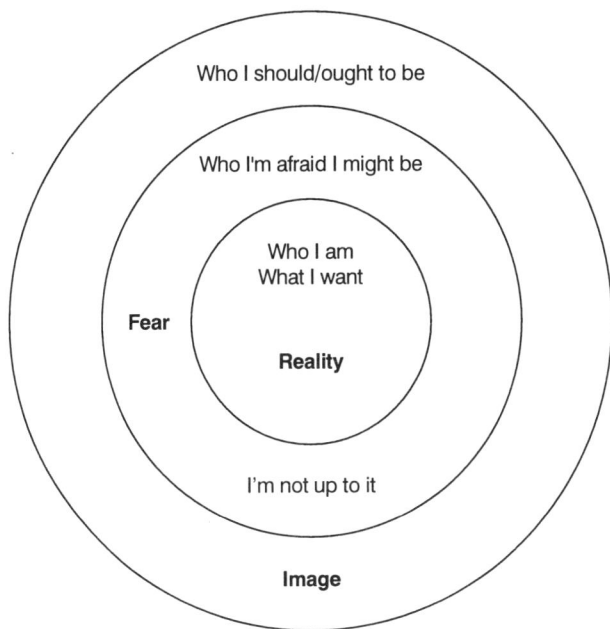

Figure 17 To learn what you want is 'selfing' not selfish

Learning to fly

Some people might perceive coaching as an altruistic exercise which benefits only the individuals being coached at the expense of the organization. The focus of coaching is on the personal development of the individual. But the reason for doing this is for the overall benefit and progress of the organization. Thus, coaching is for the ultimate benefit of the organization.

> To start off with we had a group session really to identify what were the key success factors for our business, what were the issues and concerns we had for the future...because obviously you have to tie in the personal coaching into the success criteria for the company...because it would be no use if you were having personal coaching which developed the person but didn't develop them towards the aims of the company at the same time.

The sponsor of a coaching programme, which in the case of the board would be the chairman, will invest in coaching as a method of achieving superior overall board performance. Individual directors are likely to benefit as well.

Brought into an organization in the capacity of improving overall board and company performance, the coach has a dual role. When in a coaching session, the coach must deal specifically with the client and his issues. At the same time, the coach must remember that the company has embarked upon the coaching programme for an overall purpose, such as organizational change. The coach must not lose sight of the overall objective of the programme:

> ...what he provided was the structure...because, of course, he had a responsibility for individual coaching and, to a certain extent, he had a responsibility to the organization and there is a link there.

Coaching is one of a number of tools that we use as consultants to help companies with organizational change. It gives an insight into the workings of the company. Frequently, during coaching sessions, interesting information will arise which needs to be brought to the attention of the sponsor of the project. However, it is essential that the coach separates out personal and business issues and only highlights the latter. One way to distinguish the business issues is that, if significant, they will be mentioned by more than one individual. We have found that it helps organizational learning if the coaching clients themselves recognize the business issues and raise them collectively, rather than relying on the consultant.

WHY DOES COACHING MAKE THE DIFFERENCE?

Coaching makes the difference because it pulls answers from people rather than pushing information on to them. The process ensures that clients come to rely on themselves and to recognize the great reserves of knowledge and experience that they already possess or that exist in the people around them. Generally, people's performance and ability to learn is limited by their own view of themselves. The coach will help the client to recognize self-limiting beliefs and behaviours. He will then encourage the client to use his previous experience and knowledge to learn how to tackle new business and personal issues.

Coaching is wholly non-judgemental, which means that people feel able to take more risks; to explore and practise new behaviours. The coach does not tell the client what they should or should not do. His role is to create the climate to allow self-questioning

> A lot of it was to do with self-analysis and what were my four main targets, what are the areas I wish to improve upon, how do I see myself, how do I see the business, how do I see the other people that I interact with and what am I trying to do with myself in relation to the business and other people...

In this way, the client does not just own the problems to be faced or the issues to be addressed, he owns the sense of strength and triumph from having come up with the answers and actions himself. The self-confidence that arises from realizing that you have the answers somewhere – it just takes time to find them – can be very liberating. At first the coach acts as the catalyst in the search for these answers, but in time the client learns how to access them for himself.

The personal support provided by the coach in times of extreme uncertainty can be a lifeline. Directors, particularly managing directors, can feel very isolated. They have to make difficult decisions and judgements which are often strongly criticized at the time although in retrospect they will be recognized to have been for the good of the organization.

Learning to fly

> **Example 13**
>
> At the point when we started a coaching programme in one organization the managing director had reached the point where he felt like 'giving it up'. The company had been through a dramatic change and the board had temporarily lost direction. The managing director felt a particular responsibility and extremely isolated:
>
>> I was doubting whether I had the ability of taking it forward – you've got nobody to measure yourself against. I'd got to almost an all-time low I think just by virtue of everything we had been through and I had lost confidence in my own judgment…Quite often you don't have anybody to share these things with, especially if you are a managing director – you can be a bit lonely because you've got nowhere to go.
>
> The coaching programme involved all members of the board. To begin with, the focus was on helping the board to stand back from the day-to-day managerial problems, focus on how the business had changed and understanding the implications of the change on the roles of the individuals:
>
>> I was very comfortable with it because all of a sudden it was like some help….It brought me back and it actually made me realize that what I was doing was right. I've actually realized that all the situations we've been going through are not new and everybody else has to tackle them and (the coach) has led me to other people…who've been through the same sort of difficulties.

The Benefits to the Organization

Organizations regularly spend millions of pounds as a result of structural changes and yet they rarely invest a fraction of that money in the education and development of the very directors who have to implement the changes. If companies choose coaching as a method of director development to address this, what benefits can they expect?

- The coaching process enables people to articulate and realize their personal visions which leaves them feeling positive towards the organization that has invested in them. The realization of a personal vision leads to a focus and sense of purpose not just at work but also at home which helps to reinforce the person at work. The coach helps to put a time-frame around the vision which ensures it is achieved. The tangible effects of having a personal vision include increased commitment and motivation.

- Individuals who have been coached often find that their effectiveness and level of personal organization is considerably improved. This generates more quality time for thinking. It also allows the individual the mental space to stand back from business issues which helps to put them into perspective:

I'm more stable in terms of my response to good and bad news, which occurs in everyday business life – I don't tend to peak and trough as much so my response to news is different. Now I spend more thinking time than I did before.

(At first,) all I could see was all this time had been taken out of my diary and out of my ability to do work. The interesting thing is that having the coaching and giving the time to it has made me more productive...

- A coaching programme can help to reduce the loss of good people through natural churn. We have stopped people from leaving their jobs when they felt that they were not achieving what they wanted and that leaving was their only option, usually because they did not know what they wanted. We helped them to clarify their corporate aspirations and to generate action plans for achieving these aspirations. The coaching approach is always to look for win/win outcomes for the organization and the individuals being coached. Clients are encouraged to take responsibility for their own development and their own future. It is all too easy to blame the organization for unfulfilled ambitions when, in fact, the problem is a lack of clarity about precisely what your aspirations are.
- The process of thinking through their long-term goals and aspirations sometimes means that people realize that they are in the wrong job or career. For organizations this can mean getting rid of square pegs in round holes in a positive way. The individual does not feel any loss of face or sense of failure, but rather a sense of being liberated and supported in achieving what they

Learning to fly

really want from life by their old employer. The organization benefits by the removal of the negative, distracting influence of an individual uncomfortable with their role.

- Coaching helps organizational change by facilitating individuals through the change process in a constructive and managed way. Not everyone will be able or willing to make the personal changes required by the organization and coaching can help these people realize that, for them, to leave the organization or move to a different position is a positive outcome. It helps them to let go of the past and find the courage to face a different future.
- Coaching creates change agents because in helping people to understand and manage their own personal change they are very able and well equipped to manage the bigger corporate changes and to view it as a positive and natural occurrence in life that will ultimately mean people realizing their long-term visions. People who are comfortable with personal change and learning are more likely to be able to lead organizational change.
- Coaching can help new directors to progress more quickly through induction and inclusion to performance (see Figure 11) because it provides an opportunity to identify knowledge and skills requirements.
- The coach can help the new director to answer the fundamental questions such as; 'I was a manager last Friday, I will be a director on Monday – What do I need to do differently?'
- The supportive, non-prescriptive nature of coaching improves confidence which, in turn, improves performance. In particular, increased confidence means that directors have the ability and willingness to let go of managing and they begin to address strategic issues. Many people who have been coached verify that the process helps to improve confidence levels, something vital for directors, particularly for their leadership role:

It's made me more confident – I think that's the key to it – it's the confidence of actually knowing that you can deal with it...

As a generalization, people say that if you've reached director level then obviously you must be full of confidence; but confidence can vary from situation to situation and...I found it quite useful to analyse what situations I do feel quite confident in and what situations I do not.

- Partly as a result of improved confidence and partly by helping directors to understand the processes at work, coaching can help to improve leadership skills. In a group of leaders, which is essentially what a board is, it can help directors learn when to seek consensus and when someone needs to make a decision in order to move things forward.

> **Example 14**
>
> The managing director of a company that had been through a management buy-out found himself continuously seeking consensus with his board colleagues because he was conscious that everyone was a shareholder as well as a board member. This style was against the MD's usual character, frustrating for the other board members and meant that few board decisions were reached. As a result of the coaching sessions, the MD was able to see the importance of his role as leader, even in a team of equals, to move the organization forward:
>
>> When you get to this level it's difficult because we're all employees, we're all directors and we're all shareholders. That's what the coaching has taught me – it is to try to keep these three roles apart whereas I was keeping them all interlinked because I kept thinking 'we're all shareholders so I need to pull this together in a consensus way. And I now realize that I didn't have to do that. I was trying so hard to keep it together and find a solution that was a consensus solution and, of course, it doesn't work. Well, it works in certain circumstances but it doesn't work in a lot of cases, especially if the chips are down and the pressure's on – somebody has to say 'right, this is what we are going to do.'

- Coaching groups as individuals and as a team helps build trust and improve communications. At first, the coach acts as a sounding-board for people who do not know how to relate to each other. The coach will encourage these individuals to analyse why communication difficulties exist and what they could do about them. In time, clients develop the confidence and self-understanding to confront inter-team issues by themselves. One of the bases of improved communication within teams is the recognition that people are not alike and learning to value the difference in others. The value that organizations receive from team work is that the whole is greater than the sum of the parts.

Example 15

One of our clients found the coaching process enlightening in terms of his approach to team working. He found that his coach acted as a mirror that allowed him to see himself as others saw him. He was then able to learn to change his behaviour from being generally competitive and confrontational to being more collaborative:

> (Coaching) was a very good mirror. It is very difficult to observe oneself as others see you and it was quite disturbing, in a way, the sort of insights that came out. Like, for example, I realized that I'm probably not a team player at all. If I had a choice of formulating and imposing my will on the group as opposed to seeking a consensus, I would invariably take the former route. It was in one of the coaching sessions that it became apparent that I wasn't a very good team player. And it became apparent that it was quite a small game to play and that if, for example, you are one of a board of directors, if you just seek to do your own thing as a director you will achieve certain results. If, however, you work as a board and get the whole board to think in the same way then your influence is much greater.

An Acceptable Form of Personal Development For Directors?

Directors are busy people. Any form of personal development they undertake needs to be relevant and effective. Training courses, by virtue of the fact that there are a number of delegates, have to run to a common denominator. Coaching appeals to a person's sense of self-worth because they are being given personal attention. The focus is completely on the needs and agenda, both personal and business, of the client, making it completely relevant for them and their business.

The case for coaching

Training courses are generally of one or more days in length and often off-site. Being held in blocks of two hours' duration, coaching sessions are far easier to manage in a busy person's diary and they are not taken away from the office, unless specifically requested. Meetings are held at a time and venue to suit the client: we have held sessions in airports, hotels, railway stations and so on. The only stipulations are that the two-hour session must be confidential and free of any interruptions; telephone calls and people popping into the office being the most common.

Directors can tap into the skills, experience and knowledge of the coach more easily on a one-to-one basis than on a course. They can also contact their coach outside the specific coaching sessions if they want to test an idea or talk something through with an objective third party who understands the circumstances. This can be vital, for instance, when tackling difficult relationship problems where advice might be needed quickly.

> (My coach) is a wise counsel. The fact that she's not part of this organization but she understands the operation means I frequently abuse the privilege, in a sense, and often ring up and ask, 'What do you think about this?' She always puts an external view on it. She knows what I'm like, what I'm looking for, the culture of the business and so on. It's a huge help. That's a much better help than looking to someone internally who might be too close to the business. It's invaluable because it stops me from becoming too introspective...too internally focused...makes you understand yourself a bit better.

Directors often find it of enormous help to have someone at their disposal who has no internal political axe to grind. It can be a relief to be told how a situation really is when directors tend to hear only what people feel they can tell them or what they think the director wants to hear.

It is also a relief to explore feelings, new approaches, uncertainties and problems with a peer who understands and relates to the issues but is not involved in them. The coach is a highly experienced individual who can empathize with the issues that directors experience. In many organizations, it is still seen as a sign of weakness to reveal any uncertainty, especially at director level. Coaching offers a completely confidential forum for such uncertainty to be aired. In addition, the coach may be one of the few people, if not the only person, to provide the director with feedback. We have said before how isolated the role of director can be. It is rare that a director can find people of his level who will provide him with feedback; an external viewpoint or benchmark.

> There may be times, for instance, when you are creating a wrong impression with a member of staff and you don't know about it until that member of staff has gone and then you find out that it's a part of your personality that someone else couldn't cope with – your sense of humour, or you are too sarcastic. Until someone else says, 'I can understand why that person thought that – you do have an inclination to be a little sarcastic' or whatever. And I think you might not like it but nevertheless someone needs to tell you otherwise you can lose some good staff.

Even more important than feedback, however, is acknowledgement. Often the coach will be the only person who acknowledges the director: what he has achieved, the efforts he is currently making and his future potential. The coach will acknowledge the director as a whole person. In a group of people who very often compartmentalize their lives, this can mean that directors will discuss more or reveal more of themselves with a coach than they do with anyone else, including their partner. Some may find this a threatening idea but, more usually, directors find it supportive and helpful. This is not a relationship that lasts forever. It is professional and one that ends at the point where the client learns how to coach himself and, possibly, others.

It would be a mistake to believe that coaching is a series of cosy, warm and cathartic chats: in general they are focused, challenging and hard work:

> Nobody wants to hear things that aren't positive and complimentary. I think coaching makes you face up to the realities of a situation. You might tend to think, 'I'll put that to one side, it'll go away, I'll put it in the bottom drawer – the "too-hard" box'. The fact that you've got the coaching there means that when certain issues come up I may not particularly enjoy them but you still tackle them with equal priority.

Directors find coaching useful because they can discuss real issues as they arise. Specific, relevant action plans for dealing with these issues will be developed at each session: it is action or results-driven and so helps the director to be more effective on a day-to-day basis as well as in the longer term. This approach also ensures that progress is made. Each session will begin by review-

The case for coaching

ing the progress that the director has made against the action plans agreed at the last meeting:

> A lot of the coaching process is not just about sitting having a one-to-one discussion. You sit down and explore issues but you leave that coaching session with actions that you want to carry out to deal with those issues. So the next coaching session is almost a look back at 'here's what I set out with as my objectives – how far have I got with meeting those objectives?'

Directors can find this challenging when little progress is made because the coach will ensure that the reasons for this are explored. For instance, what got in the way and why? Is there a pattern here and, if so, how will you break it? Thus, although the issues and actions belong to the director, the coach will ensure that the client matches words with deeds:

> It can be uncomfortable at times because they will challenge you in terms of 'well, you've said you want to do something, what are you going to do about it?' As straightforward as that! (It) means that you can't hide.

Coaching is, therefore, an excellent form of experiential learning. That is, it provides a method for directors to learn how to do their jobs, while actually doing them. Theory and concepts might be discussed as part of the learning process, but the main aim is to help the director determine what he will do tomorrow, how he will tackle a particular issue. As one of our clients put it:

> A good coach imparts little information. All they do is reveal what the person knows which means it is 100 per cent experiential. They are simply enabling the person to learn through their own experience and self-observation.

Helping Directors to Become Better Leaders

We have argued that directors need to be leaders. How can coaching help?

- Coaching helps build confidence and self-belief as a result of positive acknowledgement. This provides directors with the courage they need to be leaders. In particular, they have the courage to let go of the way things have been done in the past,

Learning to fly

to resist the cultural and peer pressures to conform. They are then free to create their own way of doing things rather than reinforcing processes that may have been in place for 40 years.

> **Example 16**
>
> One of our coaching clients is very different in style and temperament from the rest of the board and there is strong and yet subtle pressure on him to conform: in other words, to be like the rest of them. This would mean that a vital edge to the board would be lost in terms of a different way of thinking, a different way of approaching processes and problems which generate very creative solutions. In fact, he is very much more creative than his board colleagues. The others have all come from the industry and this individual has not. The way that the other members of the board try to undermine his approach is to argue that he does not yet know or understand the industry. This is an irrelevance but serves to undermine the individual, weaken the effectiveness of the board and slow down decision making. Coaching has helped the individual to see these processes at work and give him courage to be himself. It has also shown the other members of the board how someone different from themselves can bring benefits and help them to be more effective.

- Coaching leads to a greater appreciation and understanding of those who are different. It encourages others to look behind the obvious and look for the good or the contribution that can be made by a person who, on the face of it, might be perceived to be 'difficult' just because they have a different way of working or interacting with others:

I think that one of the big issues I had was the different types of people we had – really different types of people at the senior level in terms of their background, education, attitude – and I think my concern was how on earth this group of people was going to stand a chance at all of working together to solve anything. Even the smallest of issues seemed to be a huge problem...If I look at the business now we have made quantum leaps from where we were.

- Coaching also relieves directors of the self-imposed pressure of having all the answers. In fact, there is often no right answer for the sorts of issues, especially strategic, that directors are dealing with. There are many ways of looking at the problem and many solutions:

    It's made me realize that there is more than one way to solve the problem. I've seen so many managers who are blinkered in their approach – 'just do it this way'. (The coach) has made me realize that there is always another way to tackle a problem. There is always a solution and a way of handling it that I might not have been very good at and if I learn from that then the next time maybe I can handle the situation myself.

    It has allowed me (to) recognize the fact that there is not necessarily one solution to each issue and that there are at least two ways of doing it. Actually the real issue is about how people relate with each other as a team – that's the real issue to solving your problems and getting on with your life.

Coaching can help directors to realize that as leaders their role is not necessarily to come up with the answers themselves but to facilitate the best answers from the collective experience, knowledge and capability available throughout the company. This realization makes directors better listeners. They are then open to the view of others thereby making them more concerned managers of people – both employees and customers.

- A number of clients have commented on how using coaching questioning techniques has helped them to create better customer relationships and resolve previously difficult customer issues. This is because the emphasis moves from competition to collaboration: what can we get from this relationship rather than how much profit can I make from you.
- The better personal organization gained from coaching results in directors having time for people as opposed to tasks. The better understanding they have of themselves and the way they interact with people also makes them more willing to interact with others. These are key ingredients of leadership. Leaders lead people not things or tasks. By creating more time and confidence, leaders have the tools to improve relationships: the key to future organizational success.

Learning to fly

- The personal and professional focus gained from coaching manifests itself in a more balanced and centred person, consistent in their vision and leadership style which inspires the confidence of others:

  ...the one big difference that will make a difference in your organization (and it sounds a cliché) is the people. If you can build the right combination of people in your team you can do anything, regardless almost of those people's individual skills. If they have the right approach to the business, the goal in hand, then you can do almost anything. I think that's the single biggest thing I learned from coaching, or had reconfirmed.

What Can Be Achieved?

Below we have outlined two coaching success stories to illustrate the step-changes that are achievable and the consequential organizational benefits.

Example 17

John Brown was a senior executive of a national bank. His responsibilities were in a key operational area where morale was low. The department's credibility with the rest of the business was very poor. There had been three executives in his position during the last two years. Downsizing and restructuring had occurred. The future was far from certain. After discussion and an analysis of his situation, it was decided to start with a one-to-one coaching programme.

The first processes that were examined were leadership and the successful implementation of the operations. As a result there was an improvement in morale, effectiveness and the efficiency of the department. With the increase in confidence the employees started to put forward ideas; and initiatives were started from this part of the organization which affected the whole bank. With this success the credibility of the department increased. John Brown is now a director of the bank and chairs some of the industry's key committees. His personal influencing skills have improved and his department is now seen as one of the best in the banking industry.

The case for coaching

> **Example 18**
>
> John Smith is the managing director of a sportswear company that needed to be turned around in a very short period. Before becoming managing director, he had been the marketing director.
>
> Using coaching we helped the client to make the transition from marketing director to managing director. Within six months the company was completely restructured and the strategy revised to prevent the business going bankrupt. The focus of the business changed from manufacturing to sales and marketing. The manufacturing operation was successfully sold. Distribution and warehousing were outsourced. The new season's designs were created and a new sourcing strategy was implemented. There was a price to pay in terms of redundancies but the process was handled fairly and professionally. In addition, three of the other directors were coached.
>
> In the end, it was not the coach's ideas which turned the business around. The coach skilfully drew out the creative thoughts that existed already within the directors.

THE COACHING PROCESS

Our coaching programmes normally comprise ten two-hour sessions spread over the course of approximately a year. Initially the sessions are two weeks apart and once the programme gains momentum, the interval increases to a month. What takes place during these coaching sessions is between the coach and the client: there is complete confidentiality. If the coach thinks that there are issues that need to be raised outside of the coaching forum, particularly business-related, he will encourage the client to do this.

A coaching programme is not something that should be imposed upon someone. If a person is apprehensive at first, the aim will be to encourage the client to begin the process to 'see how it goes'. If after a few sessions the client feels that there is no benefit for him, the coaching sessions would cease. This is, however, extremely unusual.

Before the first coaching session, the client will be asked to fill out an 'Introductory Form' or 'Current Reality Statement'. The purpose of the form is for the client to establish where he is now in all aspects of his life and where he sees himself heading in the future. Just completing the form will prompt most clients to start to take an overview of their lives. Part of the purpose of this document is that it forms a contract between the coach and the client. The main aspects of the contract are as follows:

- *Purpose*
    - The purpose of the programme is to master my ability to produce results in my career and to have what I want in life.
- *Intended results*
    - Increase results in my career both generally and specifically.
    - Find out what I really want for myself.
    - Define and overcome obstacles which lie between me and my goals.
    - Manage my time and resources effectively and make the best use of my gifts.
    - Expand my sense of balance, health and wellbeing.
- *Agreements*
    - Participate in an initial series of ten sessions.
    - Allow a minimum of two hours per session.
    - Arrange the time so there are no phone calls or interruptions during the session.
    - Do everything possible to make the programme a success.
    - Allow myself to be fully supported.

The content of the Current Reality Statement belongs to the client. It is only seen by the client and the coach. It forms the basis of the coaching process. As a result of completing it and discussing it with the coach, the client will identify the aspects of himself and his life that he feels to be out of balance. The coach will challenge the client to think about:

- What do you and the company want?

- What do you need to do or change in order to achieve it?
- What is stopping you from doing it?
- What resources do you have/need to support you?
- What might you do to sabotage it?

In other words, the process starts by identifying the client's personal vision. Once established the emphasis is on setting goals and targets that ensure the vision is realized. This is where learning takes place as the client may need to do many things differently in order to realize the vision. Thus, the process of establishing and realizing a vision is the same for individuals as for whole organizations.

Right from the beginning the client will be encouraged to take ownership for his own development. For many people this can be a novel experience so the coach provides the framework for doing this. The coach will ask the client to recap at the end of the session and to agree some actions: things that he wants to achieve before their next meeting. The actions must be specific, achievable, determined by the client and sufficiently stretching to ensure learning takes place.

The purpose of agreeing actions at the end of each coaching session is to externalize clients' promises. This mimimizes the chance of clients generating an unrealistic wish-list and then feeling unfulfilled when it is not achieved.

The next session will usually start with an analysis of the action list. The review is not to judge the performance of the client but to explore what worked and what did not and the reasons behind both. Using such an approach, the coach and client can start to look at both the client's responses and the corporate processes and what is obstructing the achievement of corporate strategy.

One way the coach encourages learning is by challenging assumptions and self-limiting beliefs. Figure 18 shows how beliefs are a strong driver of our behaviour. Beliefs are something that are neither true nor false. They have been programmed into us at an early stage in life and, if unchallenged, can limit our potential. We actually seek out evidence that supports them.

Learning to fly

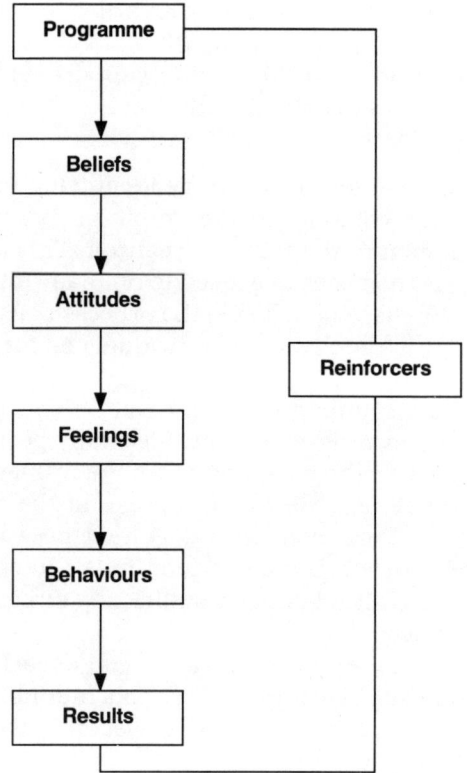

Figure 18 Beliefs are programmed into us and can be limiting

Example 19

As a boy one of the authors was told by his teachers (the 'programme') that he was not good at arithmetic. He took this on as a belief about himself and it affected his attitude about what he was and was not capable of doing. For the rest of his academic life, he avoided mathematics and sciences. His feelings about these subjects were negative which led to avoidance behaviour thereby reinforcing the 'programme'. It was only 25 years later when he was heavily

> involved in the financial aspects of an acquisition that the belief was challenged. The CEO said to him, 'You told me you were no good at maths' to which his automatic response was, 'I'm not'. The CEO simply pointed out that the evidence was to the contrary.

Learning also occurs as a result of skilful questioning techniques which help the client to articulate unconscious drivers or values at a conscious level. Realization is the first step towards change:

> It was a realization that came almost mid-sentence. You quite often find that you are voicing things and you think, 'Oh, good heavens, I don't really want to finish this sentence because I know what I'm going to say'. It was a skilful line of questioning because you don't know what you are going to say until you voice it.

Coaching Caveats

Coaching is not magic. It relies for its success on the willingness of the client to participate fully. If a client has a positive attitude from the outset and is willing to learn, the coaching process can be a powerful help. The skills and knowledge that directors need will be assimilated and practised more quickly by directors adopting a positive approach than a negative, defensive one.

> You very much get out of this what you put in and I was as wholehearted as I thought it was possible to be. If an issue came to mind I just voiced it on the basis of 'let's see what comes out' rather than consciously censoring or rationing...Some of my peers were not at all comfortable with exposing the inner man as it were, which is unfortunate...

For the organization to benefit from the directors undertaking a coaching programme it must allow them to develop and change. Coaching at an individual level will bring some insights but transformations will only occur when the environment is conducive to change, development and growth:

> But for coaching to work I think that the wholehearted buy-in of the number one person in the team is essential. If coaching encourages people to open up

and be honest and reveal themselves, if you do reveal yourself and then a dagger is plunged into your exposed soft underbelly, you ain't going to try that again!

For some people coaching is a method or style that just is not right for them. They can find the process deeply uncomfortable to the point of being threatening. Such people are unused to discussing their ideas, thoughts and feelings, especially in a work context, and do not see the relevance. The aim of the coach in these very rare instances will be to help the client get out of the sessions what they want. For instance, one of our clients uses the sessions to bounce ideas and concepts off us about how to manage change within his organization. He finds this of greater personal benefit than to discuss his personal long-term vision:

> It doesn't fit for me. You've got to understand what drives people and what influences them. I'm always cautious that when you get into those areas you are opening up a Pandora's box. Some of the personal issues can be so deep-rooted and once you've opened it up, you can't put it back in the box.

People who go through coaching, and many other forms of personal development, find that their expectations change as a result of the process. They have changed and sometimes find it difficult to explain this to others. People who experience a step-change in learning often feel frustrated if nothing around them changes. Organizations must be cognizant of this fact otherwise they will find that they develop their directors only then to lose them to other organizations.

> As soon as the individual starts unravelling his thoughts the expectation levels start to increase. When you start to get people thinking to clear their thoughts they start to realize what it is they are after…and then you are managing a different person.

Another important aspect that helps coaching to succeed is for clients to engage actively. This means becoming good coachees. We have already mentioned the importance of a positive mental attitude. There are other things that a client can do to help the process work for them. Crucially important is the ability to receive feedback. A defensive reaction to feedback designed to be constructive and facilitate learning is perhaps understandable but not

The case for coaching

very useful. Equally, dismissing positive feedback through embarrassment or modesty effectively dismisses the feedback giver. Feedback is a valuable gift from one person to another and should be treated with respect. Show appreciation for feedback received and more will be forthcoming:

> Managers who fail to receive feedback (for whatever reason) disable an important self-correcting mechanism and aid to personal productivity (Landsberg, 1996, p 14).

All successful coaching relies on an open and trusting relationship between coach and client. One powerful way for the coach to begin to gain the trust of the client will be to share something of themselves; experiences, weaknesses, worries and so on. Being a good client means playing a role in developing this relationship.

Sometimes the client will be reluctant to be coached at first. This can be for a variety of reasons and the coach will aim to ascertain the reasons and remove the obstacles. It is useful too if the client is open about the reluctance and shares his concerns with the coach. The most common reasons for initial reluctance are a fear of the level of personal learning or improvement that will result; a mistrust of the organization or the reasons for introducing coaching in the first place; a reluctance to share information with an outside 'consultant'; and a major style difference between the coach and the client. In the first three cases, the coach will explore the issues with the client immediately. In particular, the coach will stress the business requirements that have led to coaching being introduced. In the last case, the coach may suggest that a different coach takes over. However, if a client is unhappy or uncomfortable with a coaching situation, he will achieve far more by voicing and debating his concerns than by resisting the coaching process. This is because coaching is essentially for the benefit of the client.

Finally, much of the success of a coaching programme relies on the skill of the coach. This is especially true at director level. Directors do not expect to be patronized by someone who clearly cannot relate to their issues. They expect to learn from the coach and to be able to relate to him as an equal. They expect the coach to understand the particular difficulties that directors face. In addition, if coaching is to benefit the organization as well as the individual, the coach must be able to pull all the business issues together for discussion in group forums. In Figure 19 we have listed the skills that a coach of directors needs to possess. The list is extensive and necessary. It is important that companies looking to develop their directors using coaching as a method, reassure themselves of the skills and experience of the coaches, if necessary by asking to speak to other clients.

- Confidentiality
- Active listening
- Non-judgemental
- Self-discipline
- Process skills
- Self-belief
- Courage
- Empathetic
- Builds rapport
- Influential
- Objective
- Self-confident
- Has humility
- Communicator
- Experienced
- Identifies important issues
- Conceptual understanding
- Punctuality
- Questioning
- Self-awareness
- Integrity
- Able to give feedback
- Exercises restraint
- Analytical
- Professional
- Experienced in business
- Up-to-date with new ideas
- Appreciates different people

Figure 19 The skills of a coach

COACHING AS A MANAGEMENT STYLE

To be most effective as leaders of their organizations, directors need to acquire a range of influencing skills. Autocracy no longer works. Managerial and leadership styles need to be flexible to reflect the particular circumstances. There will be times when the command and control style will still be relevant, particularly during crises or where safety is in question. However, leadership today relies more and more on the director's ability to influence people. This is where coaching can help.

The coaching director makes time on a regular basis to talk to the person concerned about themselves, rather than just about the task. He recognizes, respects and encourages the person to include their total life responsibilities in work. This means acknowledging the importance of personal and family ties thus removing 'macho' management pressures such as having to be seen to be in the office

The case for coaching

before 8am and not leaving before 7pm. The coaching director provides the context for people to come up with the right answers for themselves and the business by setting the direction, giving support and then asking questions and listening to the answers. He will focus on the quality of the results achieved and will emphasize the importance of process to achieve long-term sustainable success. His aim is to inspire people, to get the best out of them and to create the atmosphere that allows them to succeed.

Quite often clients pick up the ideas and techniques that we use and absorb them into their own repertoire of managerial skills. When someone has been coached, it does tend to change their attitude towards how they interact with others. The main coaching principles that become adopted include curiosity about and appreciation of people who are different from themselves, a realization that people's limiting beliefs are the major barrier to them realizing their potential, and the use of questioning and listening to pull answers from people.

The key to introducing coaching as an internal style of management, then, is for the directors to be coached first. Without their positive experiences and, therefore, their support for the process, it can be seen as a weak and 'wishy-washy' option. There is a danger that a holiday camp atmosphere is created in the organization at the expense of real, effective work. The aim of coaching is not that everyone should feel good, although this is often part of the result; the aim is to develop self-understanding that will encourage personal learning and thereby improve effectiveness.

Once the directors have been coached, the next stage to introducing coaching as an internal process is to hold a two-day coaching skills course for the organization's principal people managers to help their transition from poacher to gamekeeper. Quarterly workshops during the first year will provide a forum for these individuals to discuss what works and what hurts. In addition, each coach should be coached by another so that a network of support is built internally.

We believe coaching to be the most effective method for encouraging personal and organizational learning. Directors who have been coached will find that they adopt certain coaching techniques naturally because their experience will have changed the way they approach other people and business issues.

Directors can begin to adopt coaching as a leadership approach to encourage organizational learning quickly and simply.

1. Initiate a coaching programme for all directors and for the board as as whole. While the cascading of coaching techniques down the organization can ultimately be done internally, directors should be coached by external consultants who have the appropriate expertise and experience.
2. Once the initial programme has been completed, set up coaching skills courses to transfer coaching skills to people who have responsibility for cascading the skills throughout the organization. To be successful they will need visible support from the board, regular refresher courses and directors to see using the coaching techniques themselves.
3. Directors help others in the organization to adopt a coaching approach by setting the example themselves. They may do this automatically or they may require some form of external personal coaching support to help them.
4. Directors can also help the adoption of coaching by talking openly about their personal experiences of being coached and what they have learned and changed about themselves.
5. Where the directors have been coached, the reaction of others in the organization is often that they would like to have the opportunity to be coached too. Directors should be aware of this and respond positively, including provisioning for such an investment. Much value will be lost if coaching is seen to be something only for the exclusive benefit of the directors.
6. Coaching criteria should also be built into the appraisal or review process, including bottom-up feedback on managers' and directors' performance.
7. Ensure that coaching is seen as an approach or style and not as a 'cure-all'. It is a method for realizing potential but it is people who resolve the organization's problems.
8. Ensure that coaching is adopted within the strategic framework of the business. Otherwise the organization might invest in the personal development of its people with only limited overall benefit for the organization.

Reference

Landsberg, M (1996) *The Tao of Coaching. Boost Your Effectiveness at Work By Inspiring and Developing Those Around You*, HarperCollins, London

Chapter 7

Coaching boards

THE WHOLE IS GREATER THAN THE SUM OF THE PARTS

As we discussed in Chapter 2, the role of the modern board of directors is complex, rapidly changing and crucial to the success of the enterprise. Its primary purpose is to ensure the long-term success of the business. In today's organizations this means that boards are responsible for corporate renewal: creating tomorrow's companies out of today's. Corporate renewal must take place within the overall framework of sound corporate governance. In other words, boards are responsible for their companies' success at the same time as complying with their legal and regulatory duties as custodians of corporations. Achieving this, sometimes apparently conflicting, balance between performance and compliance is at the heart of the function of the board of directors.

Each director on the board usually has an assigned role; non-executive director, functional executive director, managing director and so on. In spite of the apparent hierarchy that is often implied by such task devolvement, *in law all directors are equally responsible for the organization.*

In our view, the only effective way for a board to operate, given their collective responsibilities, is as a team. Functioning as a performing team allows each member of the board to fulfil a number of different roles in harmony. This is because the team has a higher order purpose that everyone has agreed collectively. Each member also understands his and everyone else's unique contribution to bringing about the higher order purpose. So, the team has an objective to reach which all the directors are equally responsible for achieving. This will usually be the vision or overall strategic direction of the company.

Where a board is not operating as a team, the overall objective can get lost in the pursuance of the directors' personal or functional objectives. Thus the business of the board can be, and often is, a fight for airtime between the different functions. There is pressure in non-team boards to conform in behaviour. Difference is seen as something at best to be ignored and at worst to be eradicated. Overall board performance among non-team boards relies on a strong chairman to pull together the disparate functions and manage conflict. As the relationships between directors are essentially competitive, there is an incentive for directors not to be open, especially about mistakes or weaknesses. More importantly, the focus on functional areas rather than the bigger picture of organizational direction can severely curtail board performance. The emphasis is on the short term and the distinct elements of the business. This narrow focus may mean that market trends and their effect on the long-term success of the business may be missed. This can mean that the board is not fulfilling its corporate governance responsibilities of looking after the long-term future of the whole business.

Boards that do not operate as teams will achieve some success. After all, the majority of boards are not teams: they are collections of strong, often similar, individuals. Our contention is that the board will not realize its true full potential or that of the organization unless performing as a team.

Team working is a way for the board to perform at a level above that of the individual members working separately. This is synergy: the ability of a group to achieve more by working together as a team than separately or merely as a group. We stress working as a team, which is not the same as merely putting a group of people together in the same room. Team working requires investment of time and personal commitment. Teams rely on openness and trust between members. This only comes through each person being committed to an understanding and recognition of everyone else's contribution to the task. This means that each person must share of themselves. They have to work in a more intimate way with other people than most of us are used to, or may be comfortable with. This is particularly difficult when the route to the top is so competitive since it means a shift from competitive (win/lose) behaviour to collaborative (win/win). But the rewards for coming through the sharing 'pain barrier' can be phenomenal. Not only do teams achieve a great deal, but the experience is fulfilling and energizing.

Directors that are part of a performing board or team understand their personal contribution and how it fits within the whole challenge of achieving the organization's vision. They have helped to design, and have agreed, the vision. They know what part their function must play in achieving this and are in no doubt that it is the overall vision that is the priority. This means that they can put difficult decisions affecting their function into context, rather than seeing them as failures or problems to be avoided. Finally, they know what contribution they make to how the board works together; their team role. They know that everyone is different and do not feel pressure to conform. They might be the person in the team who comes up with the bright ideas but it is someone else that converts the ideas into feasible options and someone else again who will actually ensure the feasible options are implemented.

It is the focus on a collectively agreed purpose and the explicit understanding of each member's roles and contribution that characterizes teams. And it is these features that make it so relevant for boards. How better to allow the managing director to lead a group of equals, for instance. More importantly working as a team forces the board to look at the overall strategic direction of the business. This is its higher order purpose or objective. This is ultimately what it has been appointed to do.

Coaching helps boards to work as teams. It also helps boards to clarify their purpose, to understand the business issues that they face and what they need to do to address those issues. Coaching is a method of personal and team development: a way of realizing potential in teams as well as in individuals. It differs from other team development processes in that it sets the development of the team in the context of the needs of the business and it focuses on realizing the potential of the team through the realization of personal potential. Coaching boards is a two-part process: the whole board is coached and the directors are coached individually on a one-to-one basis. We find this to be a useful approach because not everyone on the board will be at the same stage at the beginning of the development process. Personal coaching allows each person to progress at their own pace. Sometimes in team development people feel pressure to conform to a mode of team behaviour because everyone else has bought in, even though they are not yet comfortable with the concept. If left unaddressed, this discomfort will surface at some point in the future either as disruptive behaviour or in the individual leaving the team. One-to-one coaching ensures that people have the personal space to come to terms with what is required to work, not only in a team but, on a board of directors.

Coaching provides a non-judgemental, structured framework for the board to come to a collective understanding and commitment to change. It encourages a full exploration of half-glimpsed ideas and provides potentially isolated people with a sounding board. As with one-to-one coaching, the focus is on providing a secure environment that fosters confidence and self-challenging. This encourages learning and critical evaluation of existing beliefs that may no longer be appropriate. The board are then in a position to realize their collective potential and to address strategic issues. We believe that no one is in a better position, or has better collective knowledge, than the board to ensure the success of the business. Coaching helps to remove the obstacles which prevent the board from performing.

This can be a challenging process for boards. To begin with the directors are learning about each other and themselves. They learn to value each other's contribution and differences. They learn what collective responsibility actually means. In addition, coaching keeps them focused on the directorial tasks. Coaching ensures they stay focused on the strategic issues when the natural tendency is to revert to the tactical, especially when people are moved outside their normal comfort zones. When we are coaching boards we ensure that they address the *why* questions as well as the *what* and *how* questions. During coaching sessions we keep the focus on the things that the board itself has said are important and do not allow the bigger issues to go unchallenged. It is the best way we know to get boards, collectively and as individuals, to look at their development needs because it is not something imposed: we just create the space for the board to develop itself. After all, if the leaders are not trying to become better players what message is that giving to the rest of the employees?

ORGANIZATIONAL BENEFITS OF COACHING BOARDS

Coaching individual directors has significant organizational and personal benefits, as given in the last chapter. However, the organizational benefits can be even greater when directors are coached individually and as a board:

- Individual coaching sessions are set within an overall context of what the board is trying to achieve.
- The outcome for the organization is an alignment and clarity of personal and collective vision for the future direction of the organization.

Learning to fly

- Leadership from the board improves as a result of a sense of purpose, improved confidence and a consistent message from all board members.
- The critical strategic issues for the business are identified and 'owned' by the board.
- The gaps in expertise, knowledge, thinking style and approach at board level are identified in a non-threatening way and can be addressed both collectively and during one-to-one sessions.
- Personal fiefdoms, which usually exist as a result of a lack of trust between board members, are dispelled.
- Collaboration across functional areas begins as historical or political barriers are broken down.
- Boards develop the competence and confidence to direct, as opposed to manage, the business.
- Issues are identified earlier and aired more constructively by the board as a result of improved trust and collective responsibility, which has the effect of depersonalizing issues.
- A better use of language at board level helps to create a forum in which loyal opposition is encouraged, valued and respected ensuring that decisions once made are truly collectively owned.
- Boards become more comfortable with managing change as they have been through change themselves.
- Communication improves as boards exude a consistent message in words and deeds – the result of a clarity of purpose and common vision.
- Starting at board level, people become more proactive and prepared to take personal risks as listening and tolerance improves and collaborative win/win scenarios are valued more highly than competitive win/lose.
- A climate of learning is created as directors learn to 'pull' answers to problems from within the whole organization rather than feeling the need to have all the answers themselves.
- Valuing the difference in others is encouraged in recognizing how it contributes to the performance of the board and to the overall performance of the company:

> Another thing that came out for me was that I'm competitive and I quite like fighting my corner but if I encountered other people who were not competitive and didn't fight their corner I just completely wrote them off as a wimp to be trampled underfoot and ignored. Out of the coaching process it emerged

that there are some people who are incredibly competent but not competitive. Because they are not competitive does not mean that they haven't got good ideas...Different styles are all legitimate.

- Directors become role models for the rest of the organization's employees to emulate.

THE PROCESS OF COACHING BOARDS

As with personal coaching, coaching boards always takes place within a framework of organizational transformation. Coaching is a tool: a methodology or enabling mechanism for achieving personal transformation. But coaching cannot happen in isolation. The *why* needs to be established first.

We are often called into companies when they recognize that change is necessary but are not sure what the change should look like or how to go about implementing it. These companies also have often realized that at board level they do not have the capabilities or working style to achieve necessary change. Our immediate task is to facilitate the board to identify what the real business issues are: what are the real problems that need to be addressed? We will challenge the board's assumptions. Often the espoused problems mask the real business issues. The real issues are sometimes too large to grasp at first or cannot be seen by a board that has a functional, rather than strategic, focus. They 'cannot see the wood for the trees'.

The aim of this stage of the process is for the board to realize what its priorities need to be. They will identify the things that work and the things that hurt. They will also clarify where they become stuck as individuals and as a board when making decisions and implementing strategy and plans. How well does that board work together? How do the relationships between the individual directors affect the ability of the board to function as a whole? Is what the board is doing today actually tackling the business issues? What things does the board need to stop doing and what does it need to start to do? What capabilities as a board do we lack? What are our strengths and weaknesses? From such questioning the board derives an agreed and owned list of organizational priorities that need to be addressed through coaching.

At this point the coaching of directors on a one-to-one basis can begin. The directors and the coaches are clear about the company's issues and priorities. The one-to-one sessions, therefore, have a context. The aim is to help the individual director examine and improve his contribution to the effectiveness of the board.

Prior to the first individual coaching session, each director will complete a 'Current Reality Statement' which they share only with the coach. In this they can raise other personal issues that they wish to address through the coaching sessions. A difference between coaching individuals and coaching boards is that when we coach boards each director completes a feedback form on their colleagues which focuses on management style and behaviours. This information is fed into the process and helps the coaches to identify team relationship issues that need to be addressed. The process needs to be handled delicately so that it is not seen as a weapon with which to 'beat' other people. The purpose is to help personal understanding. What do my colleagues know about me that I do not see myself? What are my blind spots? For instance, I may think I am a good delegator but if the rest of my colleagues give me a low score on delegation, then this is feedback I should not ignore.

There will be ten two-hour sessions held with each director over the course of between six months and a year depending on the urgency of the organizational change. Meetings are held every fortnight initially, then monthly as the individual gains confidence and momentum. Each session begins with a review of what has happened since the last meeting, progress against action plans and any lessons learned which things worked and which did not and why. The session will then move on to any current or long-term issues that the director wants to discuss. As a result of the work done at the beginning of the process on the company's critical issues, the coaches are in a position to see where there is harmony and disharmony in the behaviours of the directors in relation to the board's objectives. As a rule, the coach will try to ensure that the individuals recognize any dysfunctional behaviour themselves.

About half-way through the ten one-to-one coaching sessions, a review with the whole board will be held. This is an opportunity to look at what has changed since the first analysis and what the priorities need to be for the second part of the process. Boards are often surprised by how far they have come even at this stage. The review also offers an opportunity for the coaches to highlight in a non-threatening manner any dysfunctional behaviour that has not already surfaced and been tackled. This can often be very helpful for moving boards forward since they are too close to the issue to see it for themselves.

> ### Example 20
>
> The directors on one board we have worked with all got on very well together, which tended to mask dysfunctional workings. They found that they were individually becoming frustrated by the managing director's apparent insistence on always reaching consensus decisions which took a long time. We were able to help them realize that to function effectively as a board they needed to be clear about their individual roles and responsibilities as board directors and employees as well as friends. In addition, we showed the whole board that the inability to make significant progress was not actually the fault of the MD but was due to an inadequate decision-making process combined with a lack of full participation on the part of the other directors. The board were then able to assess what they needed to do to change the decision-making process the better to reflect their changed circumstances.

A final review is held at the end of the programme to identify what the board needs to do to continue the progress. Throughout the duration of the whole process there will be informal quality checks: Is this working for you? is it dealing with what you want it to and are you learning? Occasionally there will also be additional review meetings held if particular issues arise that need to be dealt with as a board.

> ### Example 21
>
> We were asked to coach a board of directors of a medium-sized engineering company that had been through a management buy-out from the public sector. The directors, previously senior managers in the company, had worked closely together over the past 18 months as

the management buy-out (MBO) team. They had been a strong team united by the common goal of a successful buy-out.

The initial 'high' experienced after the success of the MBO soon faded, however. As the Human Resources Director put it:

> there was quite a bond between the senior managers. We had come through a terrific high to buy the company and when we got over the other edge of that we thought, 'crikey, what next?' We had to gear ourselves up again because we suddenly realized on the other side of the buy-out that this is just the beginning really.

The team's original purpose had been achieved and needed to be replaced. In addition, most of the members were new to the role of director and unfamiliar with the implications. They were aware that they had much to learn and that they needed to find their lost momentum quickly. The managing director felt coaching to be necessary for four reasons:

1. From my point of view, I had been a manager and director in the public sector and here I was now in the private sector with all the new pressures and new things to do. I had successfully achieved a management buy-out but it wasn't easy once we had all achieved it so it was very important that we got ourselves step-changed.
2. I was doubting whether I had the ability of taking it forward.
3. The team were pulling apart a bit and there was some doubt in my mind that we would be able to continue if we did not fix it – sort it out.
4. I am a great believer in continuing professional development it wouldn't be good enough just to say 'well, I'm now a director' and carry on as before.

The process that was used with the company was the same as that described above. There was an initial meeting with the whole board to identify the key success factors for the business, the issues and concerns for the future and what it wished to achieve in the long term. This provided the criteria for the individual coaching sessions. Half-way through the one-to-one sessions, a review meeting was held with the whole board to assess whether there was anything new that the group wanted to look at. It was also a chance for the board

Coaching boards

to reflect on what progress had been made already. They observed that the first meeting had served as a benchmark and felt encouraged by their achievement.

Through the coaching programme we were able to help the board to refocus and to regain their sense of team spirit. We concentrated on helping them to understand their roles as directors, particularly thinking strategically about the whole business rather than managing their own functions. The process helped the board to identify and resolve relationship issues and dysfunctional working practices. This has helped the board's collective confidence, vision and effectiveness. We were also able to help with specific issues such as what performance measures to give to a newly appointed non-executive chairman to ensure that he was being effective and how board meetings could be run. When asked what coaching had achieved, the managing director said:

> It has been well worthwhile and it's drawn out a lot of issues. It's made us realize things that we hadn't realized before about loyal and disloyal opposition. It's helped us to focus; it's helped us to discover that you've got to stand back a bit and direct rather than manage. And the whole team, not just me, have benefited...I think there was discomfort in the team initially because of the fact that we had to be honest with one another which is what the group sessions forced but once that had been done and things had been revealed and shared I think it was very positive.

> After the MBO we lost momentum. That's why the coaching has been so good because it's allowed us to get that momentum back. As an MBO team we worked really well together and we delivered. We got to the point of having done that and we had to run the company. That's a different scenario and we ended up at odds rather than together. There was basic disagreement or disbelief and the coaching process has allowed us to regain that ability to work as a team.

What are the Stages That a Board Goes Through?

Again it is useful to refer to the Change Model (see p. 62) that we use frequently in our work. Coaching will normally be introduced to the members of a board by one of their number, often the chairman or managing director. Some of the directors may be receptive at this

Learning to fly

stage but often the response is denial of the need for coaching – 'if it ain't broke, don't fix it'. This is especially the case for successful organizations. Resistance from the board usually comes in the form of 'we do not need coaching, but others further down the organization may well benefit'. At this point boards generally bombard us with questions to challenge our capability and experience. We share client anecdotes about how and why coaching has to start at the top of the organization, how it has worked and the outcomes. Exploration comes in the form of the directors completing the Current Reality Statements and then the coaching process begins. Commitment comes at different times for different people. Some immerse themselves from session one while others may take two or three sessions to get to the real issues.

Example 22

We were asked by the divisional director to coach the top team of a large division of a major transport company. He had realized that the division needed to change radically the way it was operating and the service that it offered the rest of the business. He was a believer in team working and felt that this approach and coaching would help his top team to manage the change process. The organizational change was eventually to affect all 5000 staff, involving some redundancies and retraining, and take several years to implement. As one of his team described it:

> We all recognized change but it was how to put change into place. Hence (the) direct reports had to start to function as a board rather than functional heads. You have to work together because you're impacting across the whole area of the business, hence the reason for trying to build an understanding among the various managers.

The response of the team members to coaching was very different. Some were enthusiastic from the start:

> ...all this just seemed another opportunity to understand myself better and, perhaps more importantly, to understand my peers; to give me some insight into how they operate and how they would see me because at the time we were operating as individuals rather than as a group and there was a certain amount of conflict between myself and the rest.

But others were initially less comfortable with the coaching concept:

> Because the group decided it was going to go down that path I said I would go with it – I was happy to participate. I wasn't. Dealing with personal issues is for me a personal issue. But what I wanted to do was to get people to understand themselves…So the dialogue with (the coach) became more about recognizing issues in a broader context and how to deal with those issues within the group.

Our first task was to help the group to work together as a team in order for it to work more as a board than as a collection of functional heads. This was not an easy process for the group who were operating within a command and control hierarchical structure. Eventually team roles were assigned and people recognized the contribution that they brought to the team.

> It allowed everybody to be an equal member at the table. One individual was 'grit in the oyster' – very black and white but very clear cut in thought process. So what we did was ascribe these roles to individuals within the team and everyone recognized their contribution.

Working more effectively as a team helped the group to implement what proved to be a significant and large-scale change programme from within. The coaching programme helped the individuals to identify and understand the processes at work when you try to implement change from within an organization and without sufficient top-level support.

> All the changes that we put in place at that time have gone right the way through. We were taking some big leaps in approach. Not all have gone as far as we would have liked. The one thing we misunderstood as a group was our group in relation to the business as a whole. We had developed ideas and thoughts the business was not able to receive which brought us into conflict.

Once coaching has been established and the whole board are committed, each director goes through a four-stage personal learning process which, for some, may be painful.

Unconscious Incompetence

This is the starting point; a bit like blissful ignorance. There is a confidence that change and growth will be a straight line process. Then, as coaching begins, it requires a client to examine themselves very closely and the realization dawns that perhaps while they know all there is to know in their functional area they have a lot to learn about becoming a director and effective leader of people.

Conscious Incompetence

This is the stage when a person confronts how much they do not know; the sense of hitting rock-bottom. This can be the result of their initial action plans being too ambitious and not being able to achieve the far-reaching changes that they would have liked to from the start. It can also come from the realization that, as a director, most change has to be achieved through others and that can be frustratingly slow at times. The continued development and success of individuals at this point relies on the skills of the coach to help them keep a sense of perspective and to acknowledge the progress they are making. The coach will help the individual to accept that slow, incremental progress has far wider-reaching and lasting results than sweeping changes that are likely to fall over at the first hurdle.

Unconscious Competence

With personal confidence restored, the coach will ensure that the client sets himself up for a win with more practical action plans, having reviewed thoroughly what did not work previously and for what reasons. Things then start to go right for the individual who begins to get results. This is reinforced by feedback from others that tells him that, not only is he getting it right, but other people agree with him, start to accept his ideas and initiate changes themselves.

Conscious Competence

This is the final stage when the individual has a process for handling different challenges and setbacks that has been proven to work consistently. He has a set of personal rules for winning.

Once it has been accepted by the board members that a coaching programme is going to take place and the principles of coaching have been explained, the feeling at the beginning of the programme is generally one of eager anticipation. The directors soon become a little uncomfortable as they begin to explore areas that they have not explored before. These will include differences in personal working style among the directors and how to give useful feedback to each other. Many directors find it difficult at first to discuss intimate personal details but the coaches will provide a safe environment that will ensure that the experience is positive. Other issues that will be explored will include individual's and the board's assumptions about aspects of the business. The aim will be to challenge existing beliefs about the business in order to open people up to the possibility of change. There may be another way of seeing the company and the way it does business. The coaches may have ideas and suggestions of their own as a result of their experience and because they have the advantage of being objective, dispassionate observers. And they may share these ideas. But their main aim will be to facilitate the board members to challenge themselves. Not only will the board begin to look at the business with new eyes, more strategically, but they will also learn the benefits of ongoing self-questioning. This is a crucial part of learning. Uncomfortable or even threatening for some at first, when people see the organizational and personal benefits that ensue, they are more likely to adopt self-questioning as a future behaviour.

One of the ways coaching helps to develop self-questioning is by changing language structure in order to depersonalize issues. There is a tendency, especially amongst people who have been in an organization for a long time, to associate themselves very closely with their job or role: I am my job. This means that when their function or role is criticized they are likely to feel it as personal criticism. This makes the possibility of constructive dialogue and change very difficult as people will act defensively and as if they are under personal attack. This is usually not the intention of the person who is being critical who will generally be more concerned with the situation or task than the person. For change to take place the person needs to learn that such criticism is about the way something is done and not about them as a person. This concept can be extended to behaviour. Behaviour is something that can be changed. However, a normal reaction when someone criticizes our behaviour is to feel defensive. Coaching provides an environment where there is no judgement. Behaviour or assumptions are seen in the context of whether they are useful for the client or holding him back. This helps people to examine aspects of themselves critically but constructively without feeling that their whole being or personality is being challenged. Again this differentiates coaching from counselling. Coaching assumes personality is fixed and helps the client learn to develop more useful behaviours. Counselling may look at the elements that have contributed to someone's personality as a whole.

About a third to half of the way through the programme, the directors will once more start to feel comfortable. In fact, they often feel encouraged and envigorated by the process. Often they feel closer to each other as people as they learn more about their colleagues. In addition, they will be clearer about the business issues and the long-term strategic direction. This better understanding of each other and sense of purpose means that they will be working better as a team. However, this is an early stage and the initial enthusiasm is likely to wear off without reinforcement and further learning. A serious challenge to the board at this stage is likely to see the directors all reverting to past behaviour patterns because the new behaviours are not sufficiently embedded.

The coaches at this stage will challenge the board again to shake the directors out of their new comfort zone. They will ask the board to consider issues that may have been mentioned previously but were not dealt with. They will also have a better understanding of the business and may challenge the strategic thinking of the board. This helps directors to realize that learning and change are not one-step processes but need to be ongoing.

Some Success Stories

The proof of the pudding, as the saying goes, is in the eating. So we will illustrate the effectiveness of coaching boards with a couple of examples.

Example 23

One of our clients is the chief executive of a medium-sized media and advertising company. Initially, we coached him on a one-to-one basis.

It is notoriously difficult to retain good people within the industry as set-up costs for new businesses are relatively low. In addition, companies do not tend to invest in development of staff. Some way through the coaching process, the three other directors on the board suddenly left the company to set up their own business. They had felt constrained and unable to fulfil their potential from the positions they were in. The defection came as a shock to the chief executive, our client.

Through coaching we were able to help him to address some of the issues that had caused the crisis as well as providing him with support at a time of extreme isolation. One of the main things that coaching was able to help him with was being able to face up to difficult decisions.

> One of my problems was always an ability to absorb as much information as I could about a particular situation and then spend too long digesting it and debating it with myself before acting on it – and there is a right time to act. One of my problems was that I don't particularly like confrontation so it is quite natural for me to shy away from confrontation. It is a big issue for me to be confrontational and solve issues and I realized I was letting certain situations go on for too long without taking decisive action.

We went on to help the chief executive to select a new board from within the organization. To help the new directors come to terms with their new role as directors and to help the board develop a cohesive approach we are now coaching the whole board. In this way we have combined director induction with team development. We believe that this coaching programme as well as the change in style and behaviour on the part of the chief executive will ensure that such a crisis is unlikely to occur again.

Example 24

Another of our clients is in the sportswear business. It has been going through a major change and has completely redefined what its business is about. Traditionally the company has been a manufacturing and sales oriented organization. It was a highly structured and formal organization run by people who had been with the business for many years. As a result they had become rather insular and defensive about change.

Learning to fly

> Change was absolutely critical as the business was almost bankrupt. We were brought in to help the board to redefine what the business was about. This led to the focus of the business being changed from manufacturing to marketing. The company is now a product design-led branded business. As well as acting as catalysts for change, our role was to help the board face the change and learn how to implement the change in order to take the business forward. This had to start at the most basic level of getting the individuals to relate to one another. This group of people was not interacting with each other as a board or as a management team. Everyone was acting as a head of department, interested only in their own environment and with very little cross-communication. The coaching process provided a mechanism for the group to start to communicate.
>
>> (Coaching) certainly achieved the initial aim which was to unhinge ourselves from our past which was very important and at least start the process of inter-relating more between each other and solve the problems and get to grips with them so that we could get things done...I think what it did was it allowed people to leave go of the side of the swimming pool. It's like everyone is in this new swimming pool and you are all hanging on to the sides saying, 'now I don't know if I can swim or not'. I think what the coaching process helped to do was to allow people to let go of the sides of the pool and swim a bit if they wished.
>
> The new managing director of the business, who had been brought in to turn the business around, found the process frustrating at first. He felt that things were not really moving forward. During his one-to-one coaching he learned that even small steps are steps in the right direction.
>
>> It has helped me in my response to situations...helped me to be more consensus-oriented whereas before I was gung ho on something that needed to be done and if you weren't clambering to my mast then you had to get off the boat. Now it takes longer, which I personally find difficult, but equally I find that if you can seek consensus on issues you can make progress last for longer before you hit the next challenge. So if you spend more time upfront you can make more progress.

There have been many such success stories. There are real benefits offered by coaching over other forms of team development. It is not theoretical. It is 'on the job' development. It is about the business issues that directors face now and learning how to handle them. Coaching is tailored to the needs of the board and the individual directors. It is not a prepared formula forced on organizations and teams. Being a director can be a lonely job and a coach will provide an unconditional ear. Sometimes people just like to sit and talk for two hours and in that talking they articulate their problems and come to their own conclusions. The coach's job in these instances is to keep quiet, to be a sounding-board. One of our clients uses her coaching sessions in this way. She has said that it is useful for her because she has no one else with whom she can talk through her issues: not her chief executive, nor her colleagues and certainly not her direct reports nor even her husband. So, coaching is a unique service: one that is far more focused and relevant to the job and the business issues than other forms of team development. It achieves real benefits for the organization from the start as it is not a generalized or theoretical approach that requires decoding or translating before it can be applied within the organization. Moreover, it is empowering because the directors are actually the people who have found the answers from within themselves. Real cultural change within organizations is, therefore, far more likely as personal change has taken place. These are the seeds of corporate transformation and long-term success.

Chapter 8

Conclusion

Learning to fly

Perhaps *Conclusion* is not the best title for this final chapter of the book since it implies an ending. Our hope is that, in fact, this point proves to be a new beginning for you and your organization. Nevertheless, it is our conclusion that boards of directors hold the key to the future success of their organizations. Truly leading and performing boards will be a source of competitive advantage for companies of the future.

Company directors are under pressure to change. They have come under the media spotlight as a result of some high profile examples of poor corporate governance, especially the undiminishing public attacks on directors' pay. In addition, companies are confronted by external market dynamics which make ongoing organizational change a necessity. So far the main response to competitive and market forces has come from the ranks of managers. Middle and senior managers have been through a painful transition period of redundancies and rationalization. They have learned the harsh realities of corporate life in the twenty-first century and are developing a new independence from their employers.

Change at board level has been at best, slow and at worst, non-existent. Directors have tended to react defensively to criticism and continue to act much as they did before. This is partly a result of the ingrained cultural norm that achieving director status means that you have 'made it' in your career – you are a success and your managerial style has been endorsed. Most newly appointed directors are unaware of the full extent of their responsibilities and receive little, if any, training. The general perception is that being appointed director is a reward for loyal service and managerial performance. There is little incentive, therefore, to change. Yet, this is precisely what directors need to do.

The long-term success of our companies relies on continuous transformation: the ability for businesses to keep reinventing themselves. The necessary ingredients for this to take place are continuous organizational learning and change. The board must develop the climate for this to take place. It is the nerve centre for all new ideas, creativity and innovation. Its role is to set the corporate vision and provide leadership – this is the essence of *directing*, something which is not done by many boards. More often than not, boards are collections of independent, strong-minded super managers. To achieve long-term success, boards need to recognize that their role has changed and adapt accordingly.

Conclusion

The role of the board of directors is complex and demanding. On the one hand it must ensure the company's long-term successful performance, while on the other this must be achieved while complying with any regulatory or legal obligations: the balance of compliance and performance. Both of these factors have become increasingly difficult to achieve. The debate surrounding corporate governance is unlikely to subside. The move towards greater transparency of corporate information, higher ethical standards and improved dialogue between companies and their stakeholders is an inevitability. Those companies that embrace this inevitability have the opportunity to use high corporate governance standards as a competitive advantage. One approach to improving transparency and dialogue with stakeholders is by developing partnership relationships, based on mutual benefit, with interested parties: shareholders, customers, employees, suppliers, the public and so on. Some people have called this an 'inclusive' approach. On the performance side, the rapid pace of change in the market environment will continue. The battle to remain competitive will not get any easier. Those companies that stand still will, ultimately, fail. Corporate survival in the twenty-first century will rely on companies staying one step ahead of their competitors by continuous innovation of products and service.

It is our belief that long-term competitive advantage through corporate transformation can only be achieved by the board of directors providing clear leadership and direction. Unfortunately this is rarely the case at present. Most boards are not performing well; they are not realizing their true potential. There is a tendency towards focusing on short-term operational issues. This is largely the result of the functional focus of most directors who see their responsibilities to their function of higher importance than the overall company picture. Boards need to develop a strategic focus. Without this they cannot provide the vision for the business which sets the direction for all to follow. In order for directors to set the example they need to become leaders. They need to be leaders in their own right and be a part of the leadership team – the board. Leadership is about providing the inspiration that energizes others in the organization to ensure that the vision is achieved. There is a deficit of leadership in our organizations presently because directors have not made the transition from managers to leaders.

Learning to fly

To become leaders and to achieve the complex tasks that are required of boards today directors need to acquire new skills. They need to develop new and exciting ways of thinking and behaving. They need to make the crucial jump from manager to leader, from operational to strategic thinker, from loner to team player and from commander to listener. Not only do directors need to develop new skills and behaviours but boards need to learn how to perform more effectively. Our belief is that the best way for boards to enact their collective responsibilities is through team working. For a group of individuals more used to behaving competitively, adapting to team working is not easy.

The future success of our organizations relies on directors recognizing the need for personal change and development, both individually and as a group. By far the most effective way to help directors develop the appropriate skills and behaviours they need is through coaching. Coaching makes the difference because it is a process that enables the individual to learn for himself. With the help of a coach the director identifies the areas in which he wishes to develop and learn. He identifies his personal vision and the goals to be achieved along the way to that vision. It is, therefore, a particularly relevant way to help directors develop themselves. Directors have acquired a great deal of knowledge and experience during the course of their careers. Coaching can help them to use this knowledge and experience to help them tackle problems in a different way.

Moreover, coaching takes place within the framework of the organization's strategy or needs. Thus, coaching can help identify and resolve organizational issues as well as relationship difficulties between directors. It can also help those directors who are 'square pegs in round holes' to realize this for themselves without a sense of failure. It offers directors the opportunity to learn more about themselves and others which is an important step in the development of teams. Coaching is a powerful way to ensure that directors as individuals and whole boards reach their full potential. The result is improved effectiveness and performance.

Coaching is a safe and structured method for handling personal change. It is, therefore, a powerful way to manage people through organizational change. In fact, although we have talked mainly about coaching in the context of directors, it applies equally well to people at all levels of an organization. The common thread is a

Conclusion

desire to learn and to realize potential. As coaching is for the individual and about the individual, most find the coaching process fulfilling and rewarding. It does not suit everyone but the exceptions are in the minority.

Coaching produces results and is good value for money. It is highly flexible and tailored uniquely to the needs of the individual. It is as effective for whole boards as it is for individual directors. It gets people to think about the way they think. It challenges people to look at their limiting beliefs and to 'push' their own particular envelopes'. It helps people to realize that the main thing stopping them from achieving everything they want is their own perception of their capabilities. During an era of organizational change that requires exceptional innovative ideas, coaching can help people to achieve things they did not know they were capable of which will, in turn, feed into the organization in terms of creative energy.

In our experience, directors enjoy the coaching process. It is fun. It is not remedial; it is for those who are already good and want to do even better. It can be applied to every aspect of a person's life and can achieve astounding as well as outstanding results. In a sense it offers directors a route to achieving their own competitive advantage. It can help to equip them with the skills, knowledge, thinking processes and attitudes that will make them the model directors of the twenty-first century.

We do not know what the future holds but we believe that coaching develops us to handle just about anything that is thrown at us. There is no right way of doing anything at the end of the day. Just because we have had experience of doing something one way this year does not mean that it is going to work next year because the chances are that everything will have changed by then. That is how it is with organizations. Coaching the directors will help them to learn to fly. Then boards will be places of outstanding leadership and performance.

Index

accountability 19, 24
adaptive work 110
AlliedSignal 126
Amnesty International 2, 13, 17
appraisal 158–9, 164, 194
Asda 46, 110, 124, 125

Bank of Credit and Commerce International (BCCI) 1, 12
Barings Bank 1, 12, 15
behaviour 143, 188, 209–10
Blair, Tony 1
'blame culture' 66
board 4, 36–74 *see also* directors
  accountability 27
  appraisal 158–9
  audit committee 90
  'business brain' 37, 82
  characteristics 38
  coaching 196–213
  collective responsibility 9, 38, 73, 88, 98, 196, 199, 218
  compliance 36, 196, 217
  composition 86, 94
  corporate governance 18–19
  corporate renewal 49, 51–2
  crises 49–50
  cycle of activities 69
  delegation 39, 71–2
  effectiveness 86
  leadership 30–31, 39, 59–60, 89, 104–5, 115, 128, 200, 217
  meetings 86
  nomination committee 91
  performance 36, 159, 196, 217
  purpose 40
  relationships 9, 27, 29–30
  remuneration committee 91
  responsibilities 15, 72–3, 86
  role of 14
  setting direction 52–3
  strategic thinking 70–71
  succession planning 72, 160–62
  tasks 68–73
  team development 149–53, 213
  team working 73, 98–9, 196, 198
Body Shop, The 48
Bossidy, Laurence 126, 127
Branson, Richard 108
Brent Spar 16
British Airports Authority (BAA) 43
British Airways 3, 57
British Gas 14
British Petroleum 110
British Rail 38
British Shoe Corporation 110
business planning 70

Cadbury, Sir Adrian 12–13
Cadbury Committee 2–3, 7, 24, 25, 31, 83, 90–91
  Code of Practice 24, 26–7, 90

Index

The Financial Aspects of Corporate Governance (1992) 12, 72, 90–91
Cambridge University 126
Camelot 43
Confederation of British Industry (CBI) 13
chairman of the board 85–7, 93, 154–7, 158, 160, 172, 196, 205
change 37, 49, 56–64, 97, 169, 176, 200, 211–12 *see also* corporate renewal
  change agents 63, 111, 112, 176
  change model 62, 168, 205
chief executive 85, 87–8
CIA Media Solutions 106
coach 113, 186, 187, 191, 202, 208, 209, 210, 213
  skills 192
coaching 5, 9, 129, 131, 149, 166–213
  action plans 181, 202
  benefits 174–8, 199–201
  boards 196–213
  caveats 189–92
  confidentiality 167, 179, 185
  'Current Reality Statement' 186, 202, 206
  holistic 170–71
  leadership 181–4, 193
  learning process 207–8
  management style 192–4
  personal development 166–7
  process 185–9, 201–5
  programme 172, 175, 185, 208
  resistance 206
collective responsibility, 112, 113, 199, 218
commercial focus 95–6
Commercial Union 22–3, 30

communication 9, 30, 56, 57, 79–80, 118, 119, 177, 200
  inter-personal skills 96–7
  non-verbal 58
  training 130
Companies Act 1985 34
company law 44
competitive advantage 2, 20, 216
Competitiveness (White Paper) 3
confidence 120
congruence 118
consultants 160, 162, 172, 173, 191, 194
continuous improvement 125
Co-operative Bank 20, 28–9
Coopers and Lybrand 141
corporate governance 1, 2, 7, 12–33, 80, 83, 90, 154, 196, 197, 217
  resistance to improvement 25–6
  ten-point action plan 32–33
corporate renewal 36, 37, 48–52, 65, 101, 169, 196
  see also change
corporate transformation 5, 213, 216
  see also change, corporate renewal,
  organizational transformation
counselling 6, 169, 210

Davis, George 109
Direct Line 48
directors *see also* board
  behaviour 99, 100–101, 105
  coaching 178–81
  communication styles 30
  executive directors 88–9
  induction 4, 8, 84, 137–8, 145–7, 156, 157, 164
  knowledge 144
  leadership 104–5, 115, 127, 144, 177, 181–4

Index

non-executive directors 89–93, 157–8
perceptions of 77–80, 81
personal development 67, 84, 138, 147–9, 158 , 166
personal qualities 77, 93–4, 143, 144
recruitment 8, 87, 155–7
remuneration 31, 84
responsibilities 15, 27
role of 3, 4, 8, 40, 67, 76–101, 196 , 217
skills 94–100
total well-being 162–3
training 4, 5, 8, 79, 143, 145–7
women directors 157
director development 134–164, 166, 174
coaching 178–81
non-executive directors 157–8
performance stages 137–43
personal development 147–9, 163–4
role of chairman 154–7
team development 149–53
training 145–7
dynamic tension 112

employee expectations 45
employee share ownership schemes 44
empowerment 113
energy map 63–4
Entirely Electronics
fictional case study 134–7
environment 46
European Union (EU) 42, 44
'exit policy' 141
'expectations exchange' 116–17
experiential learning 181
see coaching

Financial Reporting Council 12
First Engineering 106

'five whys', the 54–5
Ford 48
Foundation for Manufacturing and Industry 141–2

Gates, Bill 108, 125–6
Gillam, Patrick 110
'glass ceiling' 157
globalization 41
Green, Sir Owen 91
Greenbury, Sir Richard 13
Greenbury Committee 2–3, 7, 24, 25, 26, 31, 91
Report on Directors' Remuneration 91
GT Railway Maintenance Ltd 38–9

Halifax Building Society 124
Hampson, Stuart 13
Hanson 14
Harvey-Jones, Sir John 92–3
Hewlett-Packard 53, 54
Higgs, Derek 19
Hopkins, Ian 15

independent directors see directors, non-executive
Institute of Directors 4, 13, 48, 137–8, 143, 166–7
Standards for the Board (1995) 7, 13, 16, 36, 68, 143
Institute of Management 157
integrity 120
Interflora 21–2

James, David 110
Jennings, John 17
John Lewis Partnership 13

Kleinwort Benson 20

labour market 44
leadership 4, 8, 59–60, 104–132, 192, 217

223

Index

coaching 177
developing skills 129–32, 181–4
personality 108–9
qualities 118
styles 109–10, 120–27
team leadership 127–9
leadership contract 114–17, 128, 129
learning organization 49, 65–8, 216
learning process 207–8
Leeson, Nick 15
London Stock Exchange 12
London Underground 106
loyal opposition 114, 132, 205

Marks and Spencer 53, 54
Maxwell pension fund scandal 12
Maxwell, Robert 120
Melville-Ross, Tim 13
McDonald's 1, 46
McKinsey 2, 54
McLaughlin, Primrose 106
Memorandum and Articles of Association 94, 145
mentoring 6, 140, 149, 158
Microsoft 53, 125–6
minimum wage 44

National Lottery 43
negative information 66
'new ideas register' 68
Next 109
Nigeria 16
non-executive director 31
see also director
Nokia 65

organizational change 169, 172, 176, 218
see also change, corporate renewal

forces for, 3, 7, 41–6
organizational culture 29, 169
organizational identity 53–4
organizational purpose 54–5, 69–70
organizational structure 70–71
organizational transformation 201
outdoor 'survival' courses 151–2

partnership 29, 46
performance management 83
personal development plan 148–9, 163–4
personality 108–9, 153, 210
PIRC (Pensions and Investments Research Consultancy) 13–14, 17, 18
privatization 12
psychometric tests 152–3

Richer, Julian 124, 125
Richer Sounds 124
Royal and Sun Alliance 110
Royal Dutch/Shell *see* Shell

Sainsbury, J 46
Sale, Ray 106
Sané, Pierre 13
Sears 110, 124
Securities and Futures Authority (SFA) 15
self-actualization 170
'selfing' 170–71
self-managed learning 148
'shared meaning' 57
'shareholder democracy', 21
shareholders 2, 7, 12, 14, 20, 21, 22, 27, 76, 79, 217
Smith, Tony 106
'social acceptability' 46
social accountability 13
Social Chapter 44–5
Shell 2, 16–18, 19, 29, 46

Index

stakeholders   101, 217
Standard Chartered   110
strategic thinking   94–5, 146, 183
strategy   70–71, 81–2, 159, 168, 200, 210, 218
Sugar, Alan   108

'Tarzan swing', the   63
team leadership *see* leadership
team development   149–53
team working   38, 98–100, 122–3, 124, 177–8, 183, 197–8, 205, 206, 218
technology   42
Thatcher, Margaret   109
Toyota   53
transport   43

UK economy   4, 42

values   53–4, 55, 69–70, 104
Virgin   51, 53
vision   55–9, 69–70, 98. 111, 131, 174–5, 187, 197, 199
Viz   125
voicemail   42
Volkswagen   55

Walt Disney   54
Warwick Business School   141
Wharton Business School   21
whistle-blowers   114
women directors *see* directors
work
   performance stages   137–43
Worldwide Fund for Nature   2, 17